GW00384608

More Pembrokeshire Murders

This book brings together details of the horrific murders that John Cooper has been found guilty of. It also details in chronological order other mysterious deaths that have occurred in Pembrokeshire, Wales, UK that bear all the hallmarks of the same person.

This is my third attempt at writing this book. Friends told me that my first script was too disjointed and needed to be rearranged. Although rewritten I am sure the very same comments may be made of this version!

Cover Pictures © ITV Studios Ltd include host Jim Bowen on the TV Game Show "Bullseye" and John Cooper televised in 1989. Although trying to smile, the horror and humiliation of losing on the darts, is all too clear in his eyes. This devastating disappointment prompted Cooper to kill again.

Amazon paperback

ISBN 9781973368908

Author: JK Rogers

First printed 2017.

SECOND EDITION

MAP OF ACTUAL & SUSPECTED
MURDERS, carried out by John Cooper
During the years 1976-2008

Contents

Contents

Illustrations   Page

Some background history.

John William Cooper is one of the most notorious serial killers in Welsh History.

He was found guilty and sentenced to life imprisonment at Swansea Crown Court in 2011 for two double murders together with an armed robbery and sexual offences, all occurring in the County of Pembrokeshire, over the previous 25 years. Born in Milford Haven in 1944, John William Cooper, was a married man with a son and daughter. By the time he was captured and found guilty of the four murders he was a grandfather. Cooper led a double life. Sometimes gentle, sociable and hard working and at other times an evil, aggressive and extremely violent killer. Mr Gerard Elias QC, prosecuting, said the murders involved 'the use of cold, calculating violence and the merciless execution of four people for pitifully small financial gain but to ensure their silence.' Cooper's crimes centred on Milford Haven, a cosmopolitan town on a tidal waterway of the same name, situated on the extreme south westerly corner of Wales. It is a major town next to the Pembrokeshire Coast National Park, an area of outstanding natural beauty some 200 miles due west of London.

Timeline

John William Cooper was born 3rd September 1944 at Milford Haven. He had elder brothers, one of which has now died and was described to me as a particularly 'hard man'.

In 1956 at age of 12 he knew his future wife, Patricia.

Cooper went to Milford Grammar School but left when he was 15 years of age. Before he was 18 he is said to have been sent to Borstal Reform School for an armed assault. Possibly with a knife attack on a Police officer, but this is not confirmed.

In 1961 He trained as an upholster's apprentice and was a good furniture carpenter.

On July 11, 1966, he married Patricia and they lived in a Council house in Howarth Close, Milford Haven. They had a son, Adrian, in January 1967 and a daughter, Theresa, the following year.

1976. Cooper worked with a fencing contractor, erecting sheep fences. 7th December 1976 An elderly couple were found dead in their farmhouse in Llangolman. 1977-1978 Cooper worked as a Welder's mate at Gulf Oil Refinery.

1978 Cooper wins a Cross the Ball Competition in the newspaper. On a 50 pence bet he won the jackpot prize and scooped a massive £90,000 cash (equivalent to over £500,000 in today's money). He had an option of an additional £4,000 or the Austin Rover Princess car, he chose the car. Cooper gave a gift of £1000 pounds each to nine family members and took his wife off for a "no expense spared " holiday in America, where a relative of his wife lived. Properly invested the prize money should have set Cooper up for the rest of his life. Wisely, he did buy some property where he wanted to live just outside Milford Haven. 1978 Cooper bought Big House Farm in Rosemarket and five and a half acres of land. He left the Gulf Oil refinery and started working his land as a smallholding. He grew barley, stabled horses, had poultry for egg production and reared a few calves.

About 1982 Cooper sold Big House Farm to the manager of the Lord Nelson Hotel, Milford Haven. To complete the settlement for Big House Farm, he was given a 24 ft cabin cruiser and a diamond ring.

Cooper lost his driving licence for a year (?) around 1979 and did a lot of cycling around Rosemarket and Johnston . With the money from Big House Farm, Cooper purchased Valetta Villa a seafront house in 1982. The house was situated near Llanstadwell Church and overlooking the estuary between Hazelbeach and Neyland. The 24 foot cabin cruiser he had acquired he put on a swinging mooring directly in front of his house. Although he did little diving he did have SCUBA diving gear on his boat at this time. His son Adrian, aged 15, left home and changed his name to Andrew. About 1984 His family moved into 34, St Mary's Place, Jordanston. A tenant labourer with Mike Richards of Jordanston Farm. . 22nd December 1985 Scoveston Manor murders.

Cooper was again raising calves, growing barley, selling eggs and stabling horses. Meanwhile, Pat Cooper continued her activities as a seamstress. 1987   Patricia Cooper was kicked by a horse and she almost died. Flo's husband Archie Evans dies.

4th February 1989 "Flo" Evans found dead at Rosemarket.

29th May 1989 Cooper goes to ITV studios be filmed for the Darts "Bullseye" program . He admits that he has an unusual hobby. 24th June 1989 TV darts Bullseye Show screened to the public, showing Cooper on television

29th June 1989 Dixon couple murdered near Little Haven. 5th July 1989 Wedding ring of Mr Dixon sold by Cooper to a Jeweller in Pembroke. 5th July 1989 Dixon bodies were discovered.

1990's Cooper's grand daughter Gina is being treated for meningitis, Cooper was involved with many hospital visits.

21st September 1992 (Monday) Tooze farmhouse had a shotgun stolen from it.

7th July 1993 (Monday) Harry and Megan Tooze executed at Llanharry, South Wales.

April 1995 Jonathan Jones wrongly convicted of Tooze murders. Released from prison after an Appeal in 1996

6th March, 1996. Teenagers at Mount Estate fields, Milford Haven attacked, two girls sexually assaulted by Cooper. 1st November 1996 Sardis armed robbery. Sardis Trail shotgun found in hedge.

21st January 1998 - John Cooper was charged at Haverfordwest Police Station with a number of burglaries and an armed robbery (collectively known as Operation Huntsman),

29th January 1998 Ballistic and Forensic experts search Cooper's house to look for stolen goods and evidence. They take away nearly 600 items and 160 sets of keys from the cesspit. . The Duck Run Shotgun and cartridges were found in Cooper's garden.

10th December 1998 Cooper sent to prison for 30 burglaries and the Sardis armed robbery, he served 10 years of a 16 year sentence. House burglaries around Milford Haven dropped by 90%.

2005 Operation Ottowa commenced reviewing forensic evidence of the Pembrokeshire murders. About 2007 Pat Cooper begins living at Spring Gardens, Letterston, near Fishguard. In December 2008 Cooper moves into the Letterston bungalow, where his wife was living. On the very first night reunited his wife, Pat suddenly dies.

2nd January 2009, Cooper starts living alone at Letterston.

13th May 2009 Cooper is arrested near his house in Letterston. He remained in custody until his Swansea Crown Court eight week trial in 2011.

26th May 2011 Cooper (aged 66) is found guilty of four murders, one rape, one sexual assault and five attempted armed robberies. Cooper is serving his four life sentences.

October 2012: Cooper appeals Dixon's murder convictions.

November 2012: Judge rejects appeal.

2015   An appeal has been declined. Cooper will be in prison until his death.

The Author, Cooper and SCUBA Diving

I was living in North Pembrokeshire when the news broke of the Scoveston Murders. Like thousands of others both professional and amateur, I put my brain to work as to how to identify the killer or killers. I had not forgotten the previous incident of an elderly couple killed mysteriously in a fire in Llangolman and had always presumed some connection. I soon realized that it was likely to be someone living locally and that if I got too close to them, I too may become their next victim. With reluctance, I decided not to get actively involved. Besides there were many professionals who were getting paid to do just that, who understandably, had far more information about the crimes than me. I had to remain aloof. I may have played darts against him in the Bridge Inn, Haverfordwest. If it was him, I know I lost the game, and I was a reasonable player. I certainly met him on another occasion. I was giving a slide lecture evening talk at the Nelson Hotel in Milford Haven, the date evades me, but it was about 1989. Cooper was the first to approach me after the talk while I was packing away the slide projector. He asked me what I knew of the treasure ship SANTA CRUZ. Although an extremely relaxed social setting, the conversation soon became confrontational. He could not understand why I had not mentioned this treasure ship within my talk on local shipwrecks, as though I was deliberately hiding what I knew about the ship. During our short conversation he said he dived. This surprised me because I thought I knew all the divers in Pembrokeshire at the time.

I had been actively involved with sub-aqua training in the County for over 20 years and knew all the amateur divers who were within the three local Sub Aqua Clubs. I asked him what his name was and he said his name was Cooper which I misheard as Hooper. I went on to tell him about the how the surname Hooper, probably arrived in Pembrokeshire. A survivor had come ashore from a shipwreck near West Dale giving rise to the headland name of Hooper's Point. He soon corrected me and repeated his name was Cooper and not Hooper. As I had not seen him before I wanted to know who he dived with, to which he mentioned the Fire Brigade Rescue Service. Some of the Milford members were standing next to us who quickly and venomously denied that he was part or anything to do with their group. These others did not want to be associated with Cooper and I was soon getting the same impression. Within five, minutes I recognized that Cooper had a hostile and confrontational nature and was not one to socialize with. I have talked to many others who have had similar experiences. After only a brief meeting with Cooper, they too wanted to disassociate themselves from him finding his attitude intimidating, confrontational, aggressive, or even violent.

Cooper did very little diving
Cooper was known to have some diving equipment on his small cabin cruiser, but he did not do much diving. In reality he may have dived in Pembrokeshire only a handful of times. As far as the author can determine Cooper never did any formal sub-aqua training, certainly not with anybody within Pembrokeshire. He may have gone on a PADI introductory course on his holiday in USA in 1979, introducing him to the basics. At the time Cooper said he was into sub-aqua the author was carrying out a considerable number of dives throughout Pembrokeshire and never once came across him at the dive sites. In the pubs near Milford Docks where Cooper would sometimes frequent were the "Crayfish Divers". They risked their lives daily outside Skomer and the Hats and Barrels commercially diving for crawfish. I used to call them the "Kamikaze Boys" as the diving they did was definitely suicidal. The money they earned was phenomenal, they were experienced and competent divers but they

Cooper would not have been able to join them as he was not up to their diving competency. Also living locally they may have known too much about him and not want to be near him.

Cooper at this time may have had his flush years from his big win and not considered this. If he did any diving at all it was when he had his small boat and only pottered about the Haven. There is another reason I believe Cooper may not have done much diving. He always had a thick moustache. Any diver will tell you that it is a hindrance having a moustache as there is tendency for the water to fill the mask when underwater because it is hard to get a good seal under the nose if there is any thickness of hair in the way. If I was doing a lot of diving and wanted a beard as well, I would always shave the area under my nose and keep the beard away from my upper lip. Diving instructors who have full beards and dive a lot are familiar with the problem and sometimes grease the moustache to help form a better seal before their dives. If Cooper had not had much training and yet dived with his thick moustache he would get water ingress into his mask all the time. Divers with moustaches often have to suffer water seeping into their mask. This is most distracting even for experienced divers. For a novice like Cooper it would have been most annoying. This may have been one reason why Cooper did not do as much diving as he liked others to believe. Recreational divers did not consider it macho, unusual or anything to boast about. If you were were a pretender then the sport may appear to have these attributes. On his TV debut, Cooper is talking about an unusual hobby, he, for sure, is not talking about SCUBA diving, but something far more sinister. At the time of the show most divers would not refer to their sport as SCUBA, that term being applied about a decade before. Also what intrigued me was that the host of the show, reading from his script board, prepared through the contestants own submissions, talked about Pembrokeshire's underwater profile being as varied in depths as the cliffs and mountains seen above the water. These are the same words as I had used in my lecture some months before. It may have been a complete coincidence but Cooper added this snippet to his submission to get on the TV show, filling out his application about the same month as my evening talk.

Doubles Fixation.

Throughout his murderous career Cooper has secretly revelled in being a DOUBLE murderer using a DOUBLE barrelled shotgun. Cooper may have had a fixation about TWO's and DOUBLES. Any regular darts player is always thinking of doubles and the game itself used to be DOUBLE IN, and DOUBLES OUT. Competition darts is now played as starting on 501 and ending in a DOUBLE. Many people are convinced that Cooper was also involved with a double murder in Llanharry. The two persons shot had the very surname of Tooze, pronounced the same as TWO's. Many serial killers, including a recent American serial killer, seem to have a fixation over certain surname initials or words. For Cooper it could be Double or Two's. I have not checked but I bet the Milford Haven and Neyland bookmakers will tell you that Cooper's bets were Win Doubles, Daily Doubles, Dual Forecasts or accumulating bets that Doubled.

Cooper and his Shotguns.

At one time Cooper did possess a shotgun licence, but for many obvious reasons he failed to renew it when the time came for its renewal. Renewal, although relatively simple would involve dealing with the Police who then have an excuse to visit his home. It also involves a fee and an identifying photo and compliance in keeping the ammunitions and weapon under lock and key.

Cooper from the mid 1980's was a prolific burglar. The Police regarded him as a **one person crime wave** who robbed and burgled houses on an industrial scale. Cooper has never admitted any of his crimes so we do not know the true extent of his burglaries, robberies, rapes or murders. What we do know are the crimes he has been found guilty of. He served ten years in jail for the violent armed robbery in Sardis and no less than thirty robberies or burglaries. This is a large number considering he did not admit to any of them. Because Cooper used to rob from farmhouses and remote rural house and cottages, he would have come across many shotguns. His son told the Swansea Crown Court that his father regularly used shotguns.

Cooper was familiar with taking guns apart and adapting them. A shotgun was found on his premises in 1989 that had been adapted in the following way; It had been sawn off, to make transportation and concealment better. It had been painted black to stop it shining in the dark, and camouflage it in the shadows. It had large clips and a cord attached to it. This enabled the gun to be carried over one shoulder under his coat to conceal it. The clips look larger than need be; but there is a reason. As Cooper always wore wool gloves the clips needed to be large to open them up with a gloved hand. Cooper needed to unclip it with gloved fingers while it is on his shoulder so it is ready for immediate use. If he could not unclip it, he would have to remove one arm from his coat to use the gun.

Police discovered another shotgun in a pipe under the garden at Cooper's house. It was found in two halves showing that Cooper was familiar with taking guns apart. He was questioned by the Police, after two guns had been found in or near his home. One Police question was "How much do you know about firearms?" Cooper answered "I'd say I know a fair bit." Cooper explained that he had previously been a shotgun license holder and had been shown handguns and rifles by a relative in the USA. (This might have been when he went on holiday to America in 1978).
As the discovered shotgun was found buried two feet beneath mud where the ducks roamed in the garden of 34 St Mary's Place, it shows the thoroughness of the search by the Police. The shot gun had been dismantled, oiled and carefully wrapped in a black plastic bag inside a length of plastic soil pipe. The Police considered that it had been hidden with an intent to re-use it at a future date. At the same time, the cartridges for this gun were found in a plastic box, identified as coming from Scoveston Park, the scene of one of Cooper's double murders. This Belgium made gun is the one used in the teenager attack at the Mount Estate. The gun discarded by Cooper after the Sardis Burglary is the one used in the Dixon Murders.

The following photographs show two guns belonging to Cooper.
The upper gun, was used by Cooper in the Dixon Murders and the Sardis
Armed Attack.
Cooper has shortened the barrels and fixed a cord to the gun, enabling it
to be carried hidden beneath his coat. Large clips to the cord mean the gun
can be quickly taken off his shoulder without having to take off his coat first.

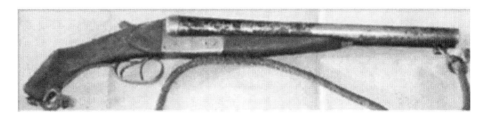

The lower picture shows the Bruno or 'Duck Run' gun. When
Cooper was in prison, the Dyfed Powys Police carefully searched his
house and garden. This gun was found carefully hidden inside a pipe
under two feet of mud in Cooper's back garden. This is the gun
Cooper used during the Teenager Attack.
Photographs ©Dyfed Powys Police, © Wales News Media © Legakis Photography/Athena.

Under oath, Cooper's son, Adrian, explained various interesting facts about his father and his guns. Cooper had a locked up garden shed where he had a workbench with a vice. One day his son saw a shotgun in the vice, the barrels of which were being sawn off. He also described to the Police that his father often went out at night, all dressed in black, with a shotgun under his coat. Cooper had various shotguns at the time, according to his son, he had at least one side by side shotgun and one up and over shotgun.

The two boy teenagers in the Mount Estate attack were able to describe in detail Cooper's gun. During this rape attack Cooper had placed the gun on the ground with the torch on top to show the barrels pointing at the terrified victims. They described the gun as being a sawn off shotgun, a side by side shotgun that had a cord lanyard and clips on it. This gun was stolen from an unoccupied detached bungalow in Castle Pill Crescent on 1st March 1996. It had been adapted by Cooper in just four days. It was probably being used for the first time by him to perform this attempted armed robbery on the teenagers.

Although Cooper would have had many shotguns there were only three guns discovered by the Police near his house. These are the gun found discarded by Cooper after the Sardis robbery, nicknamed by the Police as the Sardis Trail Gun, the gun found hidden under mud in his garden, called the Duck Run Gun and another found in a nearby hedge which was a single barrelled shotgun.

On page 67 of Steve Wilkins book "The Pembrokeshire Murders, Catching the Bullseye Killer" a statement is made that the gun found under mud, referred to by Police as the 'Duck Run Gun", was stolen by Cooper in a robbery on 1st March 1996 Despite the serial number having been ground off, it was later identified by the owner as the one he had lost in the burglary. The owner explained that ammunition had also been stolen from his locked steel gun cabinet.

This is a BRUNO shotgun with a short stock, ideally suited when the barrels are cut down for hiding underneath a large coat.

There is a good chance that this is the gun that his son Adrian, saw being adapted in Cooper's workshop.

After the Scoveston Murders, no spent cartridges relating to the murders were found and no guns were discovered in the burnt out manor house. There had been a robbery at the manor some weeks before the murder and a shotgun had gone missing. There is a good chance that it was Cooper who stole it and he took the same gun on his return to the Manor, with robbery, rape and murder on his mind. Both of Cooper's guns had been modified with a screw and washer fixed to the butts to enable a lanyard to be fixed. There was a missing bolt on one of the guns and this bolt was located in the same workshop as Cooper was known to take his shotguns apart. It was only after one of the interviews with Cooper that the Police looked in greater detail at the Sardis Trail Gun. At the end of the trial when Cooper was jailed for 30 burglaries and the Sardis armed robbery, the Judge ordered that the Sardis Trail Gun be destroyed. This was never done. When Cooper realized at an interview nine years later that the Police still had the gun he was very agitated. This gun consequently became a vital piece in the jigsaw of the later evidence against Cooper for the two double murders. After the finding of the shotgun known as the Duck Run Gun, Cooper explained to Police that this gun had been given to him by someone else who had asked him to get rid of it by throwing it off the Cleddau Bridge. Cooper said he was actually on his way to do that when he spotted a Police car and returned to his house and buried it instead. This statement by Cooper, actually brings up another interesting fact about his knowledge, or perhaps lack of it, concerning the Cleddau Bridge. Basically one would think throwing a gun off the Bridge is an easy way of getting rid it. However, there are CCTV cameras that can record any activity on the Bridge and for someone committing suicide or somebody discarding illegal items, they are likely to be recorded on video. In reality, putting yourself on camera is a rather dumb thing to do. Cooper should have known of the CCTV cameras on the Bridge, but perhaps this story suggests that he did not have this knowledge. Cooper did live within sight of the Cleddau Bridge when he owned Valetta Villa near Llanstadwell Church in 1982.

It was a different gun that Cooper used in the Dixon Murder. It has been modified by shortening the barrel and being painted black. This is the one with large clips holding a cord to enable Cooper to undo one end of the cord with gloved hands so that the gun can be slipped off his shoulder without taking an arm out of his long coat. In 2011 there was a gun amnesty where the public can hand in guns to the police with no questions asked. Each time an amnesty happens, about twice as many guns are collected than expected. In Dyfed Powys region 847 guns were handed in. In April 2003 a similar exercise collected a frightening number of weapons. In Pembrokeshire someone is three time more likely to hold a shotgun licence than the UK average. This is not surprising as it is a rural area with many small farm holdings. Recent figures show there are 17,000 shotgun licence holders in Dyfed Powys for 36,000 weapons, ie about two guns to each licence holder.

While the Dixon Murder investigation was in full swing, a black bag with a jacket and a shotgun was found on the roadside at St Brides. Curiously, even according to Wilkins book, time was not spent by the Police in tracing the owner or who had placed it there. It seems to me very unusual that someone would leave the bag there, anticipating the Police would find it. My second thought, could this have been deliberately put there by Pat Cooper (Cooper's wife) or his son as a major clue to help the Police catch the killer? The other possibility is that Cooper himself put it there, with clothing and a gun belonging to someone else to thwart the Police investigation. I would think it most bizarre that a local person, knowing that the Police were studying that whole area would have deposited a bag there when they obviously needed a car to get there. Perhaps it was a single barrelled gun and not the type thought to have been involved with the murders. I am sure the Police themselves may have considered all these theories. During the year before Cooper's Trial, he continually shouted at the public, "that they must hear the 'evidence'". This so called 'evidence' was not brought up in his eight week trial, triggering an outburst by Cooper after the Trial that the Jury had not had all the facts.

To what Cooper refers, we do not know but I have even wondered if he planted a shotgun in St Brides for the Police to find, planting 'evidence' onto someone else. If this was the case then Cooper could not be the one to first mention it to his Defence or to the Police as they would understand his ploy. We know that his son Adrian, admitted driving his father's car to Little Haven after the murders, or that is what was told to Police. Whatever the true circumstances, I for one, would be interested to know why the Police detectives did not investigate this gun and clothing in greater detail.

Hallmarks of Cooper.

Described by the Judge as "evil and predatory", and described by his son as "very, very strong and extremely aggressive", we know that Cooper kept himself very fit. He was an expert with shotguns and lived and worked outdoors. He prided himself as a survivalist, studied the SAS Survival Manual and was one of the most prolific burglars Wales has ever seen. He had a gambling streak which when his prize money ran out, caused him to seek easy money through robberies. Because he liked the thrill of taking risks, his crimes developed into stalking lone females and entering their houses both to commit robberies and to obtain sexual gratification. At every occasion of coming across house keys he would take them, knowing that he could rob that house without having to break and enter. More importantly he could enter the house silently and without raising suspicion and then be able to surprise or control the occupant where and when it suited him. Anything covert that he could do without being caught, would interest him. The bigger the risk the more it excited him. He is thought to have watched houses at Mastlebridge and Hazel Grove for hours during 1983. Many of these houses have back rooms and bathrooms that can be viewed from a thick hedgerow. At night he could hide there in his dark clothing just observing. When he wanted to leave he can depart over fields back to his house without anyone seeing him. He may have studied houses with single female occupants. As the bedrooms are not overlooked by other houses, women may dress and undress with curtains open and the lights on, thinking they are not being observed. Cooper would know all such bedrooms and the times of the show. He would also take a mental note of when the occupants were away from the house, understanding their routine to know when he can rob it.

Stupidly people would lock the house and put the key under a flower pot, not realizing that someone like Cooper is both watching and waiting for them to leave the house and go shopping for an hour. Not only does Cooper now have a key to get in, but he can keep it for a future occasion as well, often without the owner even being aware that they had lost a key. Cooper was always well prepared, and needed to be in complete control at all times.

The crimes for which Cooper has been convicted all possess one or more of the following;

Controlling the victims by aggressive actions and voice.

Controlling and frightening victims with a shotgun or a knife. Tying up the victim with hands behind their back using cord he has brought with him.

Demanding money or its whereabouts with violence and threat of death.

Hitting the forehead of victims with the butt of his shotgun.

After domination of the victims to carry out rape or a sexual assault.

To kill at point blank range with a double barrelled sawn off shotgun.

To try and hide the bodies or to cover his tracks to make detection harder.

To remove all spent cartridges from the scene of the crime.

To wear dark coloured gloves and a balaclava.

To deny everything and have good alibis ready.

Of the convicted crimes there is a common theme of sexual gratification as well as robbery. On each occasion that we know of the victim's head has been deliberately covered. This happened to Mrs Clarke in the Sardis Robbery where a pair of jeans was put over her head. Also Helen Thomas at Scoveston, where a man's shirt was put over her head. In the teenager rape, her top was pulled over her head. It is also another act of control and domination. Cooper is less likely to be recognized and he is less likely to get bitten by his victim, also any shouts or pleas for help will be muffled. If his intention is to shoot them afterwards then he does not want to see their eyes or want the victim to see his. Covering the face and eyes is not in keeping with most males during sexual intercourse.

Part of the sexual stimulation for a man is to see the eyes and face of the woman during sex. To see how she is reacting, her agony or enjoyment when she climaxes. With Cooper we know from all his known cases that he always covered the head of his victims. Although we cannot deduce, we can surmise that there is a possibility he performed necrophilia ie persisted with his sexual gratification after the victim was dead. On every case Pathological evidence says it was not conclusive that he had sex with his victims. Even in the case of the teenage rape, no semen was ever discovered. It may be that rape did occur but to leave no evidence Cooper would pull out and ejaculate elsewhere.

It is well known that serial killers, immediately after killing are in such a heightened state, that sexual acts are also committed. These may not have been the initial intention, but it is all part of the same human response of being satisfied at an achievement. It would appear in Cooper's case both robbery and sex were paramount in his intentions. If anything went wrong or he thought he thought he was going to get caught then he would kill as well. When the Police were investigating the Milford Teenage attack, they considered if the group had not been so cooperative and passive, he would have killed all of them. Cooper's dilemma here was that there was more chance of being caught by the Police if he had killed them all.

Cooper often had dogs and sometimes more than one. I surmise that he had dogs for a variety of reasons. One reason was that they acted as guard dogs to his house. If dogs barked he knew there was someone or something unusual going on. A stranger could be visiting or a fox could be after his chickens. There are two other good reasons for him having dogs. He, like many in South Wales may have had a small dog to help locate or dig out badgers, or even fight badgers. Another good reason was that if he was caught with his gun out at night it would look like he was out for rabbits. It was his alibi. On the occasion of the Teenage Attack, the victims thought that the dog with Cooper belonged to him. I am sure it was, as he also had a 12 v lamp with him. Not mentioned in Wilkins book is the fact that the gun Cooper had with him that night he had only stolen days before. It was stolen from a house not far from the Mount Estate and only four days before. In that time he had adapted it by putting on straps to carry it under his coat. I think it was the first time he was taking it out. He wanted to try his new gun out, so he took his dog along with him, having the alibi of rabbit shooting at dusk. The excitement of trying out his gun made him hyper aware and want to take more risks so he attacked five teenagers, dominating and controlling them all.

Some general characteristics of Cooper

Around 1982 Cooper developed the habit of going out at night and looking for houses to burgle. At the time he had bought a waterside property near Llanstadwell Church. Nearby were fields and hedgerows and above Hazelbeach was an estate of new bungalows being built, named Hazelgrove. At the rear of the bungalows is a Bridle Path and a remote footpath leading to open fields. This was a favourite haunt of Cooper both when he was living at Valetta Villa and for a number of years afterwards. Four of these newly built bungalows were burgled, the footpath and fields behind them being very convenient for Cooper to observe, rob and disappear. This location is about ten minutes walk along a built up road directly from Valetta Villa where Cooper lived in 1983. If he went the longer route using hedgerows, paths and fields, it would be a 15 minute minute walk, completely out of sight of any houses.

It maybe at this time that Cooper developed the idea of stealing house keys. If Cooper had spent hours watching these houses during the day and at night, he would realize that many of the retired occupants would have a weekly routine. Leaving the house for a few hours on a certain day of the week, but often be at home each night. Being new, the front doors were often securely locked. However they were all built with double glazed sliding patio doors at the rear which could be quickly prized open. Cooper even made a special tool to prise these open. At least three of these Hazelgrove bungalows were victims of Coopers robberies, being entered by patio doors. Other properties are thought to have been burgled using keys to external doors collected by Cooper on a previous visit.

A friend of mine who lived on a smallholding just twenty minutes walk away from this estate told me he suspected that Cooper stole two lifejackets from his shed. I asked him why he suspected they were stolen by Cooper. He said it was after Police had enquired if he had been burgled. At that time he thought nothing had been taken as there was no sign of a break in. Later he realized that someone had done a lot of climbing over a high fence and into the loft of a shed, ignoring three dogs on the loose. Two good lifejackets had been stolen, items that would have been useful for Cooper's cabin cruiser boat. Later this friend realized that a small chain saw had been stolen, another useful item for Cooper.

The notion of stealing keys is quite obvious for a full time thief. Many householders spend vast amounts of money putting fancy locks on their front door only to leave a key under the flowerpot outside for anyone to use. In the rural areas where Cooper usually operated there were many isolated farmhouses. Even today, farmers would only lock up at night or when it was being left for a few hours or more. For most daylight hours the farmhouse is unsecured. At Cooper's trial, the jury was shown a homemade device that Cooper had at his house. It was a tool specifically made to prise open doors and windows, in effect a well and home made burglar's jemmy. On it Cooper had put a large loop so that it could be carried over one shoulder and hidden underneath his top coat. Like his sawn off shotgun, he can carry this on its lanyard under his coat and by unhooking the clip can take it off his shoulder without removing an arm out of the coat. Cooper knew all about covering his tracks and hiding traces of his presence. So as to leave no finger prints at his crime scenes he would always wear gloves. As he operated at night and wished to stay out of sight, his gloves would always be black or dark blue, like the black balaclava he wore to hide his face. He also painted his shotgun black and possibly his bicycle too. According to his son, he went out at night, dressed all in black with a shotgun under his coat. His son also mentioned that his father could quote from the "SAS Handbook" of which he had a copy. John Cooper studied it a lot and his son said it was "his thing". Cooper also watched all the television survival Programs.

The SAS Handbook, was written by ex professional soldier John 'Lofty' Wiseman who was ex SAS (Special Air Services). It covered the essentials of survival; research, planning and equipment. Cooper was highly organized in pre-planning his crimes. The specialized equipment he carried indicated this. Having said that there are instances where things did not go according to his plans. In these instances he was likely to panic and run.

Physical attributes of Cooper

In the words of his son, Cooper was a naturally strong man, extremely fit and very, very strong. He was also loud and aggressive.

His build was stout and muscular. A large chest, and he liked to keep himself fit and healthy. He was of average height for a UK male. Since the age of 24, that is two years after he got married, he always sported a moustache. Cooper regarded himself as a bit of a local character who was well accepted. The truth was that once people had met him, they preferred to stay away from him and have nothing to do with him. One assumes because of his argumentative nature or because of his violent tempers, or perhaps both. When he served his ten year prison sentence even the other inmates could not make friends with him. In prison he has proved to be a bit of a loner. During his ten years in prison he used his carpentry and furniture skills in making chairs for the Governor. Many outdoor workers, even those that liked to keep themselves fit and healthy used to smoke. The 1980's was the decade that many smokers gave up the habit, with the constant bombardment of doctors emphasizing how unhealthy it was. I think Cooper was an addictive smoker until the night of the Scoveston murders, and then he suddenly stopped. The Police suspected a smoker to be the killer. Cooper kept fit by the very nature of his outdoor jobs, his farming, his burglaries and being on his feet all day. Some weeks after the Scoveston murders, Cooper visited a doctor with fractured ribs, something the Police considered may have happened on the murder night.

Cooper was 66 years old and a grandfather when he was sentenced to life imprisonment. He has always pleaded his innocence to not only of all the crimes in his last Swansea Trial but also to all his previous convictions for which he served nearly ten years in prison. Psychopaths frequently do not believe that they are responsible for their murders, it is always someone else's fault. Psychological profilers say he will never admit that he was a murderer and certainly never show any remorse for his horrific crimes.

A profiler used by Dyfed Powys Police said that there was three and a half years between the Scoveston and Dixon Murders and he was sure that Cooper would have committed other violent or brutal attacks in the intervening period. The death of Flo Evans came in that period. There is now every indication that Flo's death was a murder and that Cooper must be regarded as the prime suspect. Cooper, once again, probably used all his ingenuity in deceiving the detectives that it was not a murder, and he got away with it. He still has not been charged with this murder, yet it seems obvious to one and all, that Cooper killed Flo.

Recently I was talking to some retired farm labourers in St Ishmael's who knew Cooper. They had worked alongside Cooper for the same land owner. They related a story about Cooper being in the local pub on the Green. One of the farmers on leaving the pub left his house keys on the bar top. When the farmer got to his house he realized his mistake and returned 15 minutes later to collect his keys from the pub. The keys were nowhere to be found and, curiously, Cooper had also left the scene. A week or so afterwards the farmhouse to which the keys belonged was burgled. Whoever it was, and there is only one suspect, left their calling card in the bedroom in the form of faeces lying on the bed sheets. We do not know what was stolen as the farmer would not wish to report his stupidity to the Police and for fear of further reprisals from Cooper. I asked these two aged gents if they remembered Cooper as a smoker. Unfortunately they could not remember.

According to details in Steve Wilkins book, keys were found in Cooper's house that were associated with a house in Freystrop that had been burgled by Cooper. From that house a chequebook and Bank card had been stolen. Of interest is that this Bank card was used to extract money from the Westminster Haverfordwest High Street ATM machine. It was a similar time of day to when Cooper extracted money using the Dixon's bank card some time later.

Some acquired names for John William Cooper.
The Bullseye Killer, The Wildman, The Executioner, The

Game Show Killer. Apart from these names he is certainly in an elite group of murderers now serving life for their crimes in the UK. The European Court has now ruled that Lifers should not be locked up forever without any right to appeals, they say it is against their human rights. Their legal wisdom may be correct in saying the human rights of a murderer are being compromised but they are also entirely missing the plot. Such ruling does little for the families of victims and the hundreds of people that have had their human rights violated by the single act of one person taking away the life of another. I am pleased to see that in last few years this Court ruling has been modified.

Cooper and the hedgerows

Cooper was certainly an outdoors man. He was employed as a farm labourer, and was more at home outdoors than in. He preferred walking fast away from his burglaries using fields and hedgerows as cover. Within two miles of where he lived he would adapt the hedgerows and fences to make his home route easier. He cut the top strand of barbed wire fences and tied the strand back on itself to make a climbing over a sheep fence, quicker and easier.

Besides cutting fences Cooper also cut the thickest part of the hedgerow to make his own pathway through.

He also used hedge banks and hedges as hideaway places to hide stolen goods or items he wanted nobody to discover. These places were always out of sight from the nearest house. Even in the unlikely event of him being seen adapting a hedge or fence he could easily make the excuse that he was working for the owner mending fences, which was his trade. Even if the owner turned up and enquired what he was doing he could always say he was working for a fencing contractor and had got the wrong address. Cooper would probably know and recognize the owners and farmers of all the hedgerows he altered in this way. When out at night, Cooper always wore a long waxed coat. The coat itself is made of material that is resistant to being caught in hedges, and there are fabric coatings that can be applied to the coat that give it more protection from blackthorn and hawthorn hedges.

Pembrokeshire, during the 1980's and 1990's had one of the highest density of dairy cattle in Europe. Most of the fields are "sheep fenced" which will hold cattle in the summer and tack sheep in the winter months. The fence is made up stretching a meter high "Pig Netting" between 4 inch round tantalized timber posts. This is topped with two strands of tensioned standard barbed wire about 5" apart . Such a fence will contain sheep, cows, and horses (although not recommended for horses). For someone to climb over in a hurry it is both awkward and takes time. Cutting the top one or two strands of wire and tie-ing them back on themselves will make climbing over a lot easier, and yet the fence will still be sheep proof. The wearing of gloves and stout shoes makes climbing over much faster. To make climbing over a fence even easier a snip in a lower part of the fence makes a larger foot hole, enabling a large boot to make a foot step a bit higher than ground level. Such a foot-hole can still be seen in a fence at Llanstadwell that the author is convinced was used by Cooper from the time he lived in Llanstadwell to at least 5 years later when he was still committing robberies in that area. The location is in a corner of two open fields and out of sight from all houses. It is at the rear of Valetta Villa a house that Cooper lived in during 1984. The field had new sheep fencing about 1983. . The small public footpath crosses fields about 200 meters away from this corner of a field bordered by a thick hedge. In order for Cooper to get home quickly he not only cut an opening in the thick hedge but also cut the top wire on three other fences to bypass the longer path route to his house. There is also one cut on the lower squares of the sheep net wire to allow a large boot to have a good footstep in the fence about 11 " higher than the ground. Occasionally Cooper would take a dog with him and I started looking for a hole cut in the fence for his dog. It then occurred to me that he would not do this as he would not want to make it easy for a police tracker dog to follow him. Today beyond this adapted fence it is totally overgrown with blackthorn and the pathway back to Valetta Villa is now impassible. Cooper used this route from 1983 to at least 1985.

As the undergrowth behind the fence looks unkept for 25 years the author thinks this fence was adapted by Cooper in the 1980's and the route to his former house is now overgrown and Impassable. Probably last used by Cooper in 1985.

The left picture: A top wire of the barbed wire fence is cut and pulled over to allow faster access when jumping over this fence in a corner of a field. This is not far from a house that Cooper once lived in. The other picture shows one strand of the square netting having been cut about 11 inches above ground level. It provides enough space for a working boot to have a footrest. This foot rest is convenient to get over the fence in a hurry yet not large enough for the Police tracker dogs (German Shepherd/ Alsatian) to get through.

As he was found guilty of committing burglaries carried out in Llanstadwell in 1990, he is likely to have still used this route long after he had sold his house Valetta Villa. It was the most direct route to this house from a new estate being built at Hazel Grove, where Cooper was known to carry out his robberies. The barbed wires had been tied back and a passageway made through the hedge, reducing the walking route to his house by three minutes. The location is completely out of sight from all houses. When I first saw this in 1992 there was also cleared ground in the midst of a very thick hedgerow not far from the where the photographs of the adapted fence were taken. It is an unusual and remote area. I knew nothing about Cooper's activities at the time but thought it very odd to see a cleared patch of ground inside a wide hedgerow, as it also seemed to be unassociated with a badger set. It was years later did I associate this as a Cooper cache site close to Valetta Villa. 1 revisited in 2014, I wanted to look again at the area to see if there was any remaining cache of guns or hidden goods there. Unfortunately the hedgerow has been removed in the intervening years to build an agricultural store-shed. (Latitude 51.7071599 Longitude-4.9653804) The field has also been re-fenced for horses. Disappointedly I failed to find the correct spot, so was unable to confirm my suspicion that it was a secret Cooper hedgerow hiding place. I have since heard that a man that was burgled in a house at the top of Hazelbank, actually tracked the burglar through these same fields. It was this same route that alerted the Police that Cooper used escape routes through remote fields and adapted the fences accordingly. From this information, if the Police had adopted surveillance on Cooper in 1983 or 1984 (that is ten years before the Sardis Armed Attack) they would have found out that he went out three times a week with a loaded shotgun under his coat and gloves and balaclava in his pocket.

Unreported Rapes? Within the pages of Steve Wilkins book, The Pembrokeshire Murders, we learn that there were at least four women who were tied up and burgled in their isolated homes across Pembrokeshire by a hooded man with a shotgun. All these happening from 1983 to 1989, Cooper aged 39 to 45 being the number one suspect. There is real possibility that there have been other women burgled or even raped who have not told the Police, for fear of reprisals from this violent man.

Pembrokeshire, during the 1980's and 1990's had one of the highest density of dairy cattle in Europe. Most of the fields are "sheep fenced" which will hold cattle in the summer and tack sheep in the winter months. The fence is made up stretching a meter high "Pig Netting" between 4 inch round tannalized timber posts. This is topped with two strands of tensioned standard barbed wire about 5" apart . Such a fence will contain sheep, cows, and horses (although not recommended for horses). For someone to climb over in a hurry it is both awkward and takes time. Cutting the top one or two strands of wire and tie-ing them back on themselves will make climbing over a lot easier, and yet the fence will still be sheep proof. The wearing of gloves and stout shoes makes climbing over much faster. To make climbing over a fence even easier a snip in a lower part of the fence makes a larger foot hole, enabling a large boot to make a foot step a bit higher than ground level. Such a foot-hole can still be seen in a fence at Llanstadwell that the author is convinced was used by Cooper from the time he lived in Llanstadwell to at least 5 years later when he was still committing robberies in that area. The location is in a corner of two open fields and out of sight from all houses. It is at the rear of Valetta Villa a house that Cooper lived in during 1984. The field had new sheep fencing about 1983. . The small public footpath crosses fields about 200 meters away from this corner of a field bordered by a thick hedge. In order for Cooper to get home quickly he not only cut an opening in the thick hedge but also cut the top wire on three other fences to bypass the longer path route to his house. There is also one cut on the lower squares of the sheep net wire to allow a large boot to have a good footstep in the fence about 11" inches (28 cm) higher than the ground. Occasionally Cooper would take a dog with him and I started looking for a hole cut in the fence for his dog. It then occurred to me that he would not do this as he would not want to make it easy for a police tracker dog to follow him. Today beyond this adapted fence it is totally overgrown with blackthorn and the pathway back to Valetta Villa is now impassible. Cooper used this route from 1983 to at least 1985.

Some Burglaries

According to Wilkins's book "The Pembrokeshire Murders" a house in Hazel Grove, Llanstadwell was burgled by Cooper in December 1989, and keys were taken which were later found in the cesspit of Cooper's house. On 5th November 1992 another Hazel Grove bungalow was burgled with keys again being discovered in the same cesspit. On 29th October 1994 Cooper forced entry into another of the Hazel Grove properties, again taking jewellery. A similar thing happened on 31st July 1995 to another of the Hazel Grove bungalows when cash, jewellery and tools were stolen. The tools were later discovered in Cooper's house in Jordanston. I was living a mere hundred yards away from the back of these bungalows during the same years. Returning home after being at work all day I do remember entering my house and thinking some stranger had been inside. My suspicion was because of disturbed books in the living area. I looked around to see how someone could have got in. Although I used to leave a front door key under a flower pot, the front door was visible from the road and passers by. I assumed someone had entered by opening a back window and left via the same window but making it look secure on leaving. As I found nothing missing I forgot about the incident but did put an audible window alarm on the suspect window. Knowing more about Cooper and his activities in the area, I now assume it was him who had entered during daylight hours and probably taken something pocket size from my house. Only once, at another time, do I recollect seeing a suspicious trench coated stranger walking briskly up the road past my house, but I do not remember anything stolen from my property.

So many items, regarded by the Police as stolen by Cooper, were collected from Cooper's house in 1989 that they were displayed at Haverfordwest airfield so that the members of the public could see if they recognized anything that had belonged to them. Cooper defiantly told the Police that out of all the items on display only five of them had been stolen by him.

When Cooper served his first ten years of time in prison, there was said to be a 90% drop in Milford Haven burglaries. This statistic is based on the house burglaries that the Police knew about. There would have been many more unreported thefts. It has to be borne in mind that many house burglaries would go unreported, either because the house burgled had remained locked after the theft and the owner was unaware of items being stolen or the fact that they did not want to report it to the Police. Amongst the evidence given by both the Police and Cooper's own son, Cooper would store a lot of articles that he had burgled and keep them under lock and key in a store in his garden or home. His son said that he saw picture frames in a back room with people in them that he did not recognize. I am still wondering why he would collect pictures, unless they were just trophies to remember the occasion or would place the house key at the back of each frame to identify the keys. It was also common practice for Cooper to have bonfires in his back garden, burning jewellery in order to find out what was of value and what was not. His son in Court also mentioned that he once looked inside a briefcase belonging to his father and saw silver candlesticks.

What Cooper wore and carried on his sorties.

Long waxed coat Burberry Trenchcoat An ideal all weather, all situations coat. Although expensive a familiar sight in both the high street and in the country. A useful and ubiquitous coat used by farmers and agricultural workers. They are thorn-proof and a dark camouflage colour. Big pockets inside and out to carry large objects. Large collar, with a hood, to hide face from being seen. It is akin to wearing a weatherproof tent with pockets. In both summer and winter with a backdrop of a hedgerow, this coat provides an ideal camouflage.

Working boots. Probably steel toe capped and strong leather working boots . Waterproof and comfortable for walking, strong for going through hedges and stepping on barbed wire fence strands.

Torch .. Needed to operate at night and when entering houses to be burgled. Can be used to disorientate and confuse victims.

Matches ... Part of a survival kit. Needed to start a fire to get rid of incriminating evidence.

Gloves Useful when working with hedges and barbed wire. Dark gloves added to the camouflage but also avoided leaving finger print evidence. Covering his hands prevented incriminating powder getting onto his hands after shooting and also useful in picking up spent hot cartridges. It is interesting that although the gloves prevented fingerprints, the glove fibres were the incriminating evidence some 20 years later.

Balaclava ...Used to hide his distinctive hair and to cover his face. It terrorizes his victims who are more likely to obey his wishes. He gains control quicker. He is less recognisable and it gives Cooper more confidence in his role as a Commando.

Knife ...... Most essential part of survival equipment. Used by Cooper to threaten in the 'Milford Teenager attack'.

Jemmy / Burglar crowbar... Cooper had constructed his own for prizing doors and windows. A cord and clip was attached to carry it over a shoulder and under his coat.

Sawn-Off Shotgun with cord ..The cord enabled the gun to be carried over a shoulder and beneath his coat. It was carried loaded ready for use . Used by Cooper for threatening his victims to part with their money or their bank card details. He executed people if he knew they could identify him of his crimes.

Cord ...a length of multi braid rope approximately 6 to 8 feet in length with a loop tied at one end. Used to tie somebody's hands behind their back. If Cooper did not wear gloves a quicker and simpler method to tie a victims hands behind their back is to use rubber bands. The rubber band is tied over the two thumbs to secure the arms behind the back, but this is awkward wearing gloves. He may have carried two pieces of 2 meter length cord. Cord was used on at least three of his victims. It was used to tie female victims to their beds.

 Screwdriver … He may also have carried tools to dismantle his shotgun into two halves, or a screwdriver to unscrew locks and catches on hairdressing tables or windows.

Fencing pliers … A specialized tool with a spike at one end for cutting and tensioning barbed wire. It is heavy enough to use as a hammer to knock staples into fencing posts.

Wax Jacket

Sawn off shotgun

Balaclava

Gloves

Knife

Fence pliers or jemmy.   Cord   Screwdriver

Torch   Matches

When going out on his night time nefarious expeditions, Cooper like a true Boy Scout needed to be "prepared at all times". He never knew when he might need his 'survival' equipment so it is thought he carried all this gear every time he ventured out alone in the dark.

Cooper likened himself to an SAS operator or a Commando. He studied the SAS Survival Manual and adapted his shotgun and painted it black for his own purposes. His crimes were planned with cold blooded precision. Cooper was even meant to have used curry powder to stop Police dogs from following him. He probably stopped this idea when he realized that carrying it would actually help a tracker dog. Dogs sense of smell are meant to be 35 times more acute than humans. On at least three occasions Police tracker dogs did follow his scent to his house, but when questioned, like always, Cooper was adequately prepared with alibi answers.

I suspect that not enough thought goes into each and every question when Police are trying to find out facts from witnesses or suspects. For example the Police ask Cooper questions after he has been tracked to his house. Cooper, has anticipated all the questions and is fobbing off the Police with well thought out replies. These are accepted by the Police, as though they expect everyone to tell the truth. As any skilled interviewer knows, you need to prepare every question so carefully and enquire in a certain way, otherwise you will not get the correct reply or the answer you are really seeking. This is especially so with someone like Cooper who is hell bent on denials and plausible alibis. What is the point of the Police questioning thousands of people if they are given false information in their replies? The investigating team get bogged down with so many so called 'facts' that they 'can't see the wood for the trees'.

It was only later in the investigation of Cooper, did the Police interview Adrian, his son. They probably gained more correct and relevant information from Adrian in twenty minutes than they had collected from elsewhere in years. Possibly information that would have helped the Police collect critical evidence a decade sooner.

In this respect, we hear nothing in Cooper's Trial that Pat Cooper frequented the caravan site where the Dixon's pitched their tent. This fact only emerged after Cooper was convicted, by local knowledge from those that knew the family. The Police, because they never questioned Pat Cooper, never found this out.

It is easy for an outsider to be critical of any Police investigation. They do not know the protocol, the procedures and the restraints the investigation team is governed by. They certainly do not know which lines of enquiry the Police have pursued and discarded. Decisions have to be made constantly of what to do and what to investigate. The fact that Steve Wilkins, has described some of what was going on, also unleashes some of the Police failures as well as their successes.

History has shown that the Pembrokeshire Coroner has made some dubious and oddball conclusions as to the cause of death. These in themselves have helped Cooper get away with murder. However, Coroner Howells relies almost entirely on statements collected or written by Police Officers. If these statements lack fine detail, then the Coroner may make incorrect judgement as to how the death was caused.

The author has respect for the integrity, honesty and diligence of the Dyfed Powys Police Force. This is despite them hacking into my computer when I was investigating the activities of another Police Force in Wales. Why should they waste public money hacking my computer when they could simply ask me what they want to know. Why do they not want Cooper, confined in prison for other offences, to know they are investigating him? Why do they not want to talk with his wife to speed up their investigation? They are in a realm of covert activity. This delays, and spends public money unnecessarily. A sceptic would say it keeps them in a job or negates the necessity of having to write up long complicated reports.

Cooper's crimes and suspected crimes are now detailed.

Ffynnon Samson farmhouse - Suspicious double deaths
Date: 7th December 1976,
Bodies discovered 10th December 1976
Location: Ffynnon Samson, Llangolman, Pembrokeshire.
Who died: Griff (Griffith Morris) Thomas and his sister Patti
(Martha, Mary) Thomas.
Outcome: Recorded as Manslaughter and Open Verdict.

Not yet identified as a double murder but there are un surmountable similarities to Cooper involvement especially as he was working in that area.

In the heart of the Preseli hills lies the quiet village of Llangolman. The village only gets discerning visitors who pass through on their way to look at ancient standing stones and the nearby Gors Fawr circle of stones. Nearby is an isolated farmhouse named Ffynnon Samson, or "Samson's well" in Welsh. The location is just one of 236 known healing or holy wells in Pembrokeshire. Ffynnon Samson today is a well run organic farm that provides visitor accommodation. In 1976 a brother and sister lived together in the farmhouse. Griff Thomas was 73 years old and his sister Martha otherwise known as Patti, was three years younger. On Wednesday morning 8th December 1976, Griff Thomas failed to pick up his morning paper from the village. He was a placid and deeply religious man and a man of habit. On Tuesday afternoon he had called for bread at the village shop but failing to collect his morning paper on Wednesday meant there was something wrong. The following day the postman visited the farmhouse and noticed that there had been a house fire. The bodies were discovered by a cousin of the Thomas's, Emlyn Gibby, who was 54 years old at the time. The postman notified the police who arrived to find a scene of great brutality and devastation. On Friday 10th December the Police found two burnt bodies. One of Martha Thomas and the severely burnt body of Griff Thomas, amidst a burnt out room in their farmhouse. They also found the lights on in the house and the television on suggesting that events had happened in an evening.

The police immediately suspected a burglar had committed a double murder. The news that hit the Pembrokeshire community of which I had been a part for five years was " Det Chief Supt Pat Malloy, Head of Dyfed-Powys CID, said last night that one of the possibilities being investigated was that someone went to the house to rob the couple and that they were killed during the robbery." Pat Molly died aged 73 in 2003 and was author of a book about the Cannock Chase Murders, he was responsible for apprehending that murderer. In hindsight Molloy's original hunch, as to the Llangolman mystery was probably the correct one. Certainly far more plausible than the Coroner's conclusion. Especially as Emlyn Gibby, who discovered the bodies said of Griff, "a small, mild mannered chap who would never have done that." Within one week after questioning local people as to a motive some of the Police were thinking on different lines. Local people knew that the couple had money, and some thought it was hidden in the garden of the farmhouse. However thousands of pounds were found by police who then considered that robbery was not the cause of the tragic Events.

Local people said that Martha Thomas was the one that controlled the purse strings and that Griff was always complaining that he was never allowed enough pocket money. This story of bickering about pocket money became so significant that the Coroner's Court heard a hypothetical story that Griff must have murdered his sister and then fallen into a fire killing himself or committing suicide. This story even suggests that Griff Thomas in an injured state moved his sister from the kitchen into the living room before he falls into the fire. It is a story, a chain of events, requiring far more imagination than the original theory of a burglary that went wrong.

A verdict of manslaughter was given for Patti Thomas and an Open Verdict was given for Griff Thomas, who died, it was assumed by being burnt when a wooden settle fell onto him also putting a nail through his forehead.

A further consequence of this verdict was that Mr Thomas was denied a gravestone in the local Baptist Church, a church which he had been such a part of his entire life. The Rhydwilym Church, taking heed of the Coroner's decision assumed that Griff Thomas was of unsound mind, had committed suicide and also killed his sister. Therefore the Church should not condone a place of rest for him. The minister of the Church today is the Rev Jill Hailey S Harris who, in 1976 was just a child. She obviously wishes a new investigation to what happened that tragic evening, hoping that amends can be made to the history of the Church.

So what do we know of what was happening that fateful evening ? The charred bodies of two elderly people were found in the living room of their remote farmhouse. The room showed a scene of complete devastation, with broken and burnt furniture where a fire had burnt in the middle of the room. By the time the bodies were found the fire had burnt itself out and the other rooms, apart from being blackened by smoke had not been affected by the fire. The television was still turned on and it looked as the couple had been in the middle of eating a meal. The house was constructed of stone with tiled and slate floor, built about 1890. Because both bodies had been moved it was originally assumed they were murdered by more than one killer. No obvious motive for the killing was determined, although local gossip did indicate that the couple kept some money hidden in the garden. Patti Thomas was repeatedly hit over the head with a blunt instrument, at first thought to be a heavy chair, as one was found to be blood stained. It was then considered that the chair could not be used repeatedly, as it would have been too heavy. No other implement was found that matched Martha's head wounds and it was thought that such an implement was burnt in the fire. Her body had been dragged from the kitchen into the living room and placed on top of a magazine rack. Mr Thomas's cause of death was thought to be by burns. If Cooper was involved then he could have struck blows to Martha Thomas's head with the butt of his shotgun. We know that he has done this to other female victims, on other occasions.

In this instance there was no evidence of a shotgun being used and the theory of a chair being used repeatedly, by an immensely strong and violent Cooper, is far more likely. This very same chair, after being broken, could have been used to kill Mr Thomas.

One of Cooper's characteristics is to move his victims after death. All his known murder victims, once dead, have been relocated to a different position, to both hide the bodies to prolong their discovery, but more importantly to confuse subsequent investigations. This movement of bodies has certainly caused confusion in the detective Work. It did confuse as the Police originally considered there must be two killers to Cooper's crimes as a dead body needs superhuman strength to move it at all.

It appears that Mr Thomas was killed in a doorway and his body also dragged across a room and placed in the middle of combustible material. His upper body was severely burnt but the pathologist did identify that there was a nail that had penetrated his forehead. It was then concluded that this nail must have lodged in his head after death when the heavy furniture fell on top of him. It is a very far fetched conclusion. If furniture containing nails fell on Mr Thomas, then it would have maximum mass before being burnt, then the nails would not be exposed. If a burnt piece with a protruding nail fell on his burnt body it is most likely not to have much weight with it and therefore unlikely to penetrate the skull. No nail was ever found, only a wound suggesting a nail had gone into his skull.

The author suspects that the nail-like wound was the cause of death of Mr Thomas and was put there by Cooper using his fencing pliers. Cooper would always carry these in the coat pocket of his trench coat. When I had a smallholding and needed to put up sheep fencing, it was the first specialized fencing tool I bought. As they are made of hardened steel the snipping part is excellent for cutting through thick and hard wire. Much better than your average pliers.

This multipurpose tool was always carried by fencers, to cut and strain the wire and hammer in the wire staples. It is a heavy 10" iron tool with a spike at one end. A more evil hand weapon for a serial killer one cannot imagine.

.

I am confident that if the Pathologist photographs are restudied; the so called 'nail wound' to Griff's forehead is likely to look the same as if he was pole-axed with fencing pliers.

The pathologist recorded that both bodies had suffered from smoke inhalation. Looking at the carbon dioxide levels in the blood, it was concluded that Griff Thomas had died after Martha.

This means that the fire was already going before the violence started. Cooper may have started the fire to force the couple to tell him the whereabouts of any hidden money in the house or garden. In an astonishing theorized series of events aired at the inquest, and reported in the Wales on Sunday's sister paper Western Mail at the time, the jury was told: "Something must have happened between the old couple and it could have been that Miss Thomas provoked her brother by either hitting him or pulling his hair and he then he retaliated."

It was possible that Mr Thomas had provoked his sister by starting a fire. Though seriously injured, he carried his sister from the kitchen of the house into the living room where she was found sitting on a magazine rack. He could have then staggered back, collapsing in a doorway where his blood was found before getting to his feet and then either falling back into the fire or throwing himself on it." Griff and Patti had lived together for 70 years, all their lives.

All the people who knew them considered it was not in the nature of Griff to harm his sister. "He just was not capable of doing such a thing", was the general consensus of opinion. They meant both physically or mentally.

The Coroner based his opinion of manslaughter and suicide (Open verdict) on the fact that there was no evidence of anyone else being involved. The house was locked, no weapon was found and no unusual fingerprints, no substantial amount of money was taken (how does anyone know this?) the only motive in sight was one of money between the two siblings.

Some local people, including the postman, had other ideas and thought it was a double murder by an intruder. Everyone in the village who knew Griff, thought that he would never be violent with his sister, and that the circumstances were completely out of character for him. The Coroner's verdict was on 17th February 1977 and any murder enquiry was stopped from that date.

Soon after this verdict I spoke privately to Pat Malloy, the Chief CID. He was not convinced that the Coroner's verdict was correct and thought there there could still be a murderer at large in Pembrokeshire. I had to agree with him and is why I became so interested when another double murder happened in Pembrokeshire years later.

Rhydwilym is the oldest active Welsh Baptist Chapel in the world and was founded in 1668. Funds to build the first chapel were provided by the Gentleman Farmer John Evans of Llwyndwr in 1701. We know there was a chapel on the site in 1763 because a plaque on the front wall indicates that the 1763 chapel was rebuilt in 1841, and further enlarged in 1875. Griff and Patti Thomas were part and parcel of this Chapel and had been so for three score years and ten. To think that Church members believed the Coroner's judgement rather than their own is a travesty in itself but to deny the couple a burial place is an even more distressing outcome.

On the Taro Naw, a BBC Welsh current affairs TV program in 2011. Huw Absolam, a neighbour who knew the Thomas's well, was to mention that Griff Thomas was not in good health and incapable of causing that much destruction to the farmhouse, saying that his hands were arthritic and he even had difficulty in turning the pages of his hymn book. Certainly the devastation of furniture, of lifting a heavy chair to hit his sister would have been an impossibility for him.

Such aggression would be more in keeping with Cooper's violent and brutal nature.

It is heartening to see that a gravestone has now been made for Griff and Patti Thomas. This has gone some way towards justice of the case for the small community even though the true story and the killer has not been determined. At the beginning of the investigation a double murder was thought to be the most likely scenario.

Chief CID Inspector of the case Pat Malloy said that they were looking into the possibility that a robbery had gone wrong and that someone had murdered the couple. The finding of thousands of pounds at the farmhouse, helped to both support and expel the robbery theory. All the 400 fingerprints taken at the farmhouse were eventually thought to belong to the Thomas's and not to anyone else. Cooper, would have been aged 32 at the time, and probably wore gloves for his crimes at this early stage, thus none of his fingerprints would be present.

An extensive search was carried out along the country lane looking for a murder weapon. This implies that no nail was found in Griff Thomas's skull, but a hole. When nothing was found and it was then assumed that it had been consumed in the fire, indicating a chair leg with a nail. We now know that if Cooper was involved his escape from the house would have been across fields away from the country lanes and not the obvious exit routes.

Llangolman, Efailwen and the area lying to the east of Maenchlohog in 1977 was predominantly a Welsh speaking part of Pembrokeshire. John Cooper was not a Welsh speaker and would have been regarded as an outsider having come from Milford Haven.

Anywhere south of Haverfordwest was regarded by the Preseli folk as South Pembrokeshire. There were few properties for rent in that area and most tenanted places were Tithe or agricultural tenancies. Cooper is thought to have been working for a fencing contractor and living in a caravan nearby. Cooper had been married ten years and his son and daughter would be aged 8 and 9. I surmise that Cooper was living within walking distance of Ffynnon Samson. This may have been at a caravan at Trefach Caravan Site, Mynachlogddu only a few miles away.

Cooper his wife and two children had not moved to Jordanston by this time. His wife, Pat, and two children were still living in a Council House in Howarth Close, Milford Haven with his children attending school during the week. Cooper probably visited them at weekends only. This Llangolman incident happened mid week and after dark. The date is the end of the first week of December, and Cooper was probably thinking of ways to obtain money in preparation of the fast approaching Christmas.

I was living in North Pembrokeshire at the time and although I do not remember seeing newspaper articles I do remember local people talking about the fire and a burglary gone wrong adding that the couple were rich and known to hide money in their garden. Now if I heard that from local people, Cooper working in Llangolman would have heard the same story about a lot of money hidden in the garden.

At the end of May 2011 the Dyfed Powys Police having successfully put Cooper behind bars for life, started considering if other unsolved murders or crimes could be attributed to the same person. The only other double mystery in Pembrokeshire within living memory was this one at Ffynnon Samson. S4C Taro Naw program in September 2011 had comments from Dr Clive Sims about the unsafe inquest verdict and also included comments from Huw Absolam of nearby Bush Farm who knew the Thomases well, his father was their cousin.

"We couldn't believe it," says Huw Absalom "They never did anybody any harm ever. They were very quiet people who kept themselves to themselves." "It's a shame that he has been judged as a killer of his sister – a sister that he had lived with all his life. There's no way he could have done it. Absolutely no way – 100% impossible."

Cooper may have worked out beforehand a method of killing to make it look like an accident. It is not beyond reason that Cooper hit Griff Thomas on the head with a piece of charred wood that had a nail protruding. More likely the nail and piece of wood were part of the chair already in bits after being smashed onto Martha Thomas. The Forensic team said the nail was from the settle that had burnt and had fallen onto his head. Some time after the initial investigation had subsided there was a Public Auction at the Ffynnon Samson farmhouse. Everything was being sold off including the farm dog and its kennel. I attended and bought some traditional furniture. Everyone attending the auction was probably thinking the same as me, how can we ask the sheepdog what happened that night? I still possess a pine three legged table, locally called a 'cricket table', acquired that day from the sale. Eerily, it still has burn marks on its wooden circular top, whether it also has DNA of Cooper or fibres from his gloves, I do not know.

We know from the Scoveston Murders that Cooper moved the dead bodies and put combustible material around them and then diesel to burn the bodies. Because no mention is made of diesel or paraffin to fuel the fire, this may not have been done at Ffynnon Samson. The fire had virtually extinguished itself within 24 hours and the wooden beams and ceiling of the room was still in tact which may not have happened had it been deliberately accelerated using diesel or petrol. There is no mention in the Pathologists or Police report of shotgun pellets in the bodies or in the furniture or walls of the room. The body of Mr Thomas was severely burnt and only the lower portion of his legs still recognizable. His body was sitting on top of a wooden settle (bench).

Autopsies showed that both Griff and Martha had inhaled smoke before death. The wristwatch worn by Mr Thomas had stopped at 8.20 pm. We can assume the fire that consumed his body was started in early to middle part of the evening.

In September 2011 Dr Clive Sims, a forensic psychologist living in Suffolk, said on the BBC Wales program that he thought the original Coroner verdict was "unsafe" and that he thought Cooper was a likely suspect for the deaths. He added "There is an empty cash box, the bureau has been broken into, the back door is unlocked and certain aspects of it simply do not make sense". He also said that Cooper was unlikely to start such violent and brutal murders when in his forties [referring to Scoveston and Dixon murders] and other crimes would have been committed by Cooper in his earlier years.

I have often pondered why Cooper was so violent in this incident and the motive. Two possibilities arise, apart from his serial killer instincts, where motives are beyond normal comprehension. He may have heard that the Thomas's had a lot of money and some known to be hidden in the garden . To extract that information he needs to terrorize them into telling him where to look. The second motive may have been something to do with badgers. Cooper may have seen badger sets on land owned by the Thomas's and enquired if he could come on his land. The Thomas's may have refused.

Badger Baiting Every Sunday men would meet up at Penblewin Roundabout in their vehicles and drive north into the Preseli hills to hunt out badgers. Sending down terriers into the set, the dogs would corner a badger and commence barking. This alerted those above where to dig the badger out. Once caught the badger is tied up before setting their dogs on to it, for sport and gambling, and to see if their dogs have more courage than their mate's dogs. Some badgers were thrown in the back of a mini van and taken back to the South Wales valleys to be used as live bait for a bigger and more lucrative badger baiting contest.

This sport had no appeal to the animal loving RSPCA but it was the number one gambling sport for the ex miners of the South Wales Valleys. These groups were so successful in routing out badgers that they had removed all the badgers from Glamorgan and most of South Wales. This blood thirsty pastime would appeal to Cooper especially as he could get easy money from the groups by showing them where the badgers were on the Preselis. I regularly used to watch badgers at dusk in another area of North Pembrokeshire.

I was astounded when a few months later I showed the RSPCA Inspectors where some six different badger sets were. All the sets except one had been decimated by badger baiters, annihilating approximately 35 badgers. The Animal Inspectors told me they used to watch out for a dark coloured mini van. They had seen this driving from Penblewin Roundabout going north towards Llangolman. In Wilkins book opposite page 161, is a photograph of Cooper's shed at his Jordanston address. Beside the shed is a dark coloured minivan that looks abandoned. Although this photograph was taken by the Police about 12 years after the Llangolman incident, it may be the same vehicle. I have often pondered if Cooper had developed a grudge against Griff Thomas for preventing him digging out badgers on Ffynnon Samson land.

The other motive, previously mentioned, is that Cooper had heard stories that the Thomas's were rich and had hidden money in their house or garden. Cooper may have used his violence on the couple to extract information as to the hiding places. Although some money was found by Police in the house and a handbag of money was not taken we still do not know if someone took a lot of money from a cache somewhere else in the house before setting the place on fire and killing the occupants. The fact that a handbag of money was not taken, to me suggests that Cooper did find and take one of the caches of money. After the Inquest, journalists reported that the couple kept some money hidden behind the back board of a large valve radio/ gramophone player that was in their living room. This cabinet has been referred to in the newspapers as a bureau. When this was examined, the back board had been displaced and no money was present.

There is some confusion in the reporting, as to if the house was found in a locked state or not. The Coroner based his verdict on the fact that the house was fully locked. The front door was certainly locked but I believe the back door was not. A locked up house is one of the signatures of a Cooper crime.

Factors involved in a profile of this incident.
Two adults killed
A brutal attack, blood everywhere
Carried out early evening in the dark, just before Christmas
Someone immensely strong involved
Both bodies moved after death
A fire destroys vital evidence.
No incriminating fingerprints
No obvious motive
An isolated location, farmhouse surrounded by fields.
No weapon found, but the author thinks it was fencing pliers.
House locked up
A dubious Coroner's decision.

Scoveston Manor Double Murders
Date : 22 December 1985
Location: Scoveston Manor, Steynton, Milford Haven.
Pembrokeshire.
Who died: Richard Thomas and his sister Helen Thomas
Outcome: Cooper found guilty of the murders in 2011.

The weather was wet and windy and most Pembrokeshire people were quietly relaxing in the warmth of their homes for a well earned Christmas break. The date was 22 December 1985, the last Sunday and just three days before Christmas. Millions were watching a Harry Secombe show on the television. Two women were driving from Llanstadwell to Steynton direction when, through the trees they could see a manor house ablaze. They drove up the long driveway, rushed out of the car and frantically knocked on the front door as they could see flames coming out of the roof. Getting no answer they had to drive for help. It was before the days of mobile phones.

The two women drove as fast as they could to the Windsor Club in Johnston (about five minutes drive) where their husbands were, and raised the alarm with the emergency services. The Police and Fire Services arrived, but the fire had already been raging for an estimated two hours. The Fire Services used the water in the front ornamental pond as a water source to quench the flames, but the mansion was burning furiously and it was a major fire.

Fireman Richard Brock entered the building when he arrived, but the fire was extensive and the building in danger of collapse . He discovered the burning body of dead Mr Thomas on the stairs half landing and said it was covered with stacks of paper that were still burning. Divisional Fire Officer Michael Henry George then arrived after seeing the flames from his home. He had been told of one body being found and was about to enter the building but a shout went out for everyone to evacuate.

The roof and inside floors were collapsing and the building was too dangerous to enter. It was not until the following morning that the body of Mrs Thomas was found. Her body and the bed she was on had fallen through one floor and landed in the debris on the ground floor. A specialist fire investigation officer was called in to tell the Police more about the cause and where the fire had started. His opinion was that the fire had been started deliberately by sprinkling diesel over combustible materials at more than one place in the building, and then setting it alight. He said the main seat of the fire had been in Helen Thomas's bedroom but he said that there were many other places where a fire had been started. These included papers that had been packed beneath and on top of Mr Thomas's body and various sites up the wooden stairs, and deliberately at the foot of the stairs.

The manor house was a three storey mansion built of stone with wooden floors and lath and plaster ceilings constructed in Victorian times about 1860. Cooper had carefully collected combustible material and placed them strategically around the bedroom and staircase before deliberately starting the fire to cover traces of his crime. Once alight the dry combustible material inside the house of curtains, wooden furniture, wood floors and staircase fuelled the fire to its devastating conclusion. The Mansion house was gutted and

At the time of the murders it was occupied by millionaire farmers Richard and Helen Thomas. He was aged 58 and Helen was aged 54. They were brother and sister, both unmarried who lived a quiet, somewhat reclusive life. That morning Helen Thomas had attended the Sunday service at St Peter's Church in Steynton.

The Police were quick to tell the public that the two bodies had both been shot but at the beginning they were keeping an open mind as to if it was a double murder or a murder and a suicide. The Thomas, brother and sister were both well known to Cooper who was sometimes employed as a casual farm labourer at Scoveston. Cooper was known to help them in hay making when extra hands were needed. Cooper sometimes bought hay from Richard Thomas and at least one of the observed transactions turned into an argument about the price. Someone who knew both Cooper and the Thomases said that he had once seen Cooper talking to Mr Thomas about purchasing corn or hay from him. Scoveston Manor was known to have had a burglary in the weeks before the tragedy. We now know that Cooper may have possessed a key for one of the external doors of Scoveston Manor. We do not know this for certain but we do know that Cooper had in his possession a key that fitted a room in Norton Farm, a nearby farm, also owned by Richard Thomas. When Police searched Cooper's house four years later they found no less than 163 keys, (Steve Wilkins book says 503 keys, so it is assumed 163 sets of keys). Some discovered after being thrown into the septic tank and others hidden beneath earth in the garden.

Cooper was living in a house at Jordanston. Scoveston Manor was only 1.3 kilometres away across six fields as the crow flies. To get there by foot Cooper needed to cross two busy roads.
On the night in question it is assumed that Cooper left his car near the Steynton Roundabout and approached the Manor house on foot. The author believes that he did not return the same way but panicked after seeing the burning manor house and ran across fields in the opposite direction, down the fields through the trees onto the railway line.

The Manor house is only 17 minutes walk from Coopers house. He may have waited and watched for a while to see who was in the large house. He could see that Mr Thomas's car was not in front of the house or in the back yard so he knew that the house was either unoccupied or that Helen Thomas was alone. Cooper crossed the field and entered the house. His intention may have been burglary or sexual or both. It was fast approaching Christmas and extra money into Cooper's pockets at this time was going to be a bonus. Cooper was 41 years old , his eighteen year old son had already left home, unable to cope with his father's aggression. His seventeen year old daughter and his wife Pat, were both in need of a nice Christmas present from him. Coopers gambling addiction and the time of year when household bills are mounting did not help his situation. Cooper could always join the Turkey pluckers for extra income but that was hard work and not to his liking. Burglary and robbing the rich was more exciting.

Helen Thomas was alone when Cooper entered the house. Cooper may have unlocked the front or rear main house door to let himself in, with a key that he had already acquired. Helen Thomas would have been startled at his presence and even if Cooper wore his balaclava and gloves, she would have recognized the intruder by his voice. We do not know the course of events and do not know if Cooper demanded or collected money from the house. If Helen Thomas was not in the bedroom when Cooper entered the house, he forced her into an upstairs bedroom. She had her day clothes on. Cooper forced her onto the bed and then tied her to the bed with a cord he had taken with him specifically for that purpose. He tied a man's shirt over her head to either gag her or to blindfold her, or both. Mr Thomas is thought to have arrived home when Cooper was upstairs with Helen Thomas. Both Mr Thomas and his sister were to end up dead from gunshot wounds. It is conjectured that Cooper was upstairs in the bedroom with Helen Thomas when Richard Thomas returned home by car. Richard Thomas knew there was something wrong and may have seen Cooper at a lit bedroom window when he arrived.

Cooper was taken by surprise and may have tried shooting Mr Thomas from an upper bedroom while Mr Thomas was in the yard . Cooper took a long range shot at Richard Thomas, the shotgun pellets partially hitting him but also glancing past him.

This shot may have been when Richard Thomas was walking to the door of the mansion. The shot did not kill Richard Thomas but made him realize that a maniac was at large. Richard Thomas, slightly wounded, ran to the outhouse across the front yard for his safety or to perhaps get a gun or weapon to fight Cooper with. At this time Helen Thomas is thought to be upstairs on her bed, already gagged and tied. It is not known if Cooper sexually assaulted her as her body and clothing were so severely burnt in the fire it was difficult to tell. We do know from his other crimes that once Cooper has complete control of his victims there is also a sexual element to his attacks. It is then thought that Cooper pursues Richard Thomas into the outhouse door opening and shoots him in the abdomen and chest at point blank range. Cooper may have been hit in the chest by Richard Thomas in this scuffle. Cooper then runs up the stairs to the bedroom and shoots Helen Thomas at close range in the head from the front as she lies tied on the bed. Both Mr and Mrs Thomas are now lying dead, blasted to death with a double barrelled shotgun by Cooper. The outhouse doorway was splattered with blood and the Western Telegraph was to report that this blood did not belong to Richard or Helen Thomas. This statement proved to be incorrect and it was later found to belong to Richard Thomas. The Police were convinced that the intruder had been badly injured and appealed for someone who may be harbouring him to come forward. The Police had incorrectly guessed the blood at the outhouse belonged to the killer and not of Richard Thomas merely by its location outside the house, when his body was found inside the house. Despite an intensive search of the grounds, the house and the fire debris, the shotgun was never found and nor were any of the spent cartridges used in the killings.

Lead shot was found embedded in the walls of the bedroom where Mrs Thomas was murdered. Cooper was methodical in covering his steps, also shown by trying to hide vital evidence by burning the house down.

The family of the Thomas's put up a reward of £15,000 for information leading to the arrest of the killer or killers.

It was assumed that more than one person was responsible as it needed a strong individual to carry or drag a dead man across a yard and half way up a staircase. They did not know they were dealing with Cooper, very much an individual, a very powerful, fit and strong man who was also intent on deceiving their investigation for as long as possible.

Cooper then decided to hide his evidence, he collected all the spent cartridges used and also collected at least one shotgun from the house. He also finds a box of ammunition and puts them with the guns near the front door. Cooper then goes across the yard and, using a rug, hauls the body of Richard Thomas back to the house and drags him up to the first half landing on the stairway. He reckoned the best way to get rid of two murdered bodies was to burn the house down. Cooper now looked for paper and diesel or paraffin. He scattered diesel around and under the bed that had the body of Helen Thomas still on it.

He also discovered stacks of newspapers and put these under and over the body of Richard Thomas and soaked these papers with the same fuel. He then liberally sprinkled fuel all over the staircase and around any carpets he saw on the ground floor. Using a lighter or a match he then set alight everything flammable, starting upstairs in the bedroom where Helen's body was. Cooper retreated down the stairs lighting the old newspapers around Richard's body. One rug was found near Richards body that had not been burnt to the same extent as others. This may have been the rug used by Cooper to drag the body, suggesting that diesel was poured around the bedroom before Cooper collected Richards body from the outhouse.

After setting every thing alight he collected his gun, the cartridges and all the used cartridges and left the house locking the doors as he goes. The author believes that Cooper did not return to his house or car but escaped in the other direction, across two fields to the railway line. The author believes he did not return to his own house for at least two days. This is contrary to what the Police think. They believe, through interviewing Cooper's daughter that he ran home and told the family to say that he had been in his house all night. If Cooper's car was left on the roadside at the roundabout at this time, then Cooper's whole family would have guessed it was him who had caused the Scoveston Murders.

If I was looking for any guns stolen or used in the Scoveston Murder then I would search the thickets next to the railway track below the Manor. This is also where Cooper may have scratched his face and hands on his frantic escape. If Cooper was away from his family for a few days immediately after the Scoveston Murders then his wife and children would have suspected him as the offender. During the interviews conducted by the Police in June 2008, Cooper denied having been anywhere near Scoveston Park when the Thomas' were murdered on 22 December 1985. He did later admit he may have been to their home on a few occasions, the jury heard. In reality he had probably been there on at least 15 occasions. Detective Chief Superintendent David Davies, was convinced Richard Thomas would have tried to resist an intruder, on the day he was murdered, saying: "That was the type of person he was."

The Police concluded that a plastic box full of cartridges, hidden under two feet of mud in Cooper's garden was stolen from Scoveston Manor. Whether this was at the time of the murders or from a robbery some weeks before, we cannot know, unless Cooper himself is to tell us. I would guess that guns and the box of cartridges were all collected from Scoveston in the weeks leading up to the murders and not on the night of the murders. Cooper would not want to escape in a hurry carrying incriminating guns, after all he might have had his pockets full of Helen's jewellery or money.

Around Helen Thomas's body was a piece of black knotted rope approximately 3.5 feet long (just over one meter). The Police considered that this was used by Cooper to restrain her to the bed. This together with Helen's body was badly burnt in the fire and had fallen through the burnt floor to the ground floor room below. Cooper is thought to have brought this rope with him for such an occasion; it was one of his hallmarks. Although a lot of fire debris had fallen on the length of rope the fire had failed to consume this remaining part. The length of the original rope was thought to be about 6.5 to 7.5 feet (over 2 metres) long.

When the Police raided Cooper's home, four years later, they discovered numerous pieces of cord and rope in his garden shed. Many of these had loops at one end, I assume a bowline loop not a eye splice. It reminded the Police of the cord they had seen used by Cooper to tie Sheila Clarke to her bed.

Thus the Police were of the opinion that these were adapted by Cooper who carried one or two with him with the intention of tying up his victims. By preparing the loop beforehand Cooper only needs to secure one end of the rope on itself or to a bed to tie up a victim. This makes the whole operation much quicker and simpler especially as he wore cumbersome gloves.

Was Cooper a smoker?
Amongst the many pieces of evidence that I expected to hear at the Swansea Trial, but was entirely absent, concerned cigarette butts. The Police, soon after starting their Scoveston investigation, discovered in a nearby hedgerow a large amount of cigarette ends. They came to the conclusion that these cigarettes were discarded by someone who had hid in the hedge secretly spying on the Manor House nearby, probably for hours, on the night of the murders or some time before. A big thing was made in the newspapers about these discarded cigarettes as it was one of the few things that could be associated with the perpetrator. The hedge location was in an ideal spot for observing who was entering or leaving the front of the Manor House. The Police kept some of these cigarettes. We know that DNA from the saliva on a cigarette butt can identify a killer. But nothing is heard of cigarettes in the evidence against Cooper regarding the Scoveston Murders at his trial or in Steve Wilkins's book. There are a variety reasons why these are not mentioned. a) the cigarettes may have been DNA tested but found to be smoked by someone other than Cooper. b) The Police did not pursue this line of investigation, c) the cigarette butt evidence had been lost over the years or d) it was all a hoax deliberately conceived by Cooper himself. The author is of the opinion that the cigarettes were smoked by Cooper but he quit smoking the day he knew the Police were looking for a smoker! No mention is made in Wilkins book of these cigarettes or if the Police spent any time in ascertaining from others if Cooper was a smoker at the time of the Scoveston Murders. Considering such a big thing was made of it in all the newspapers a week or so after the murders, this I find, is somewhat surprising. I suspect that over the years the Police got bogged down with so many documents and files, that the obvious was ignored. This surely alone could have been a big nugget of evidence that Wilkins was looking for all along.

Cooper put all his cunning into his murders and it is not beyond belief that Cooper put the cigarette butts there himself. It may have been a clever plot by Cooper, if he was a non-smoker, to deliberately collect butts and place them in the hedge to fool the Police that a smoker was involved. The smoking then non-smoking theory, is intriguing and I think a very important part of the Cooper investigation. But not a word of it is made in his trial. The whole cigarette scenario could have been a very clever ploy by Cooper to deceive the Police. All such deceit helped in his lack of detection for so long. Cooper himself says that he doesn't smoke, but he may have been a smoker at the time of the Scoveston murders and stopped smoking immediately after, because he knew the Police were looking for a smoker. The hedge location is near the bypass road and in direct line between Cooper's house and the front elevation of Scoveston Manor. It is not far from where cars used to stop at the side of the road. A motorist cleaning out the ashtray of his car may have thrown them into the hedge. The scatter and the ash should have dismissed this theory before the Police contacted the newspapers. Not one word is mentioned at Cooper's Trial, nor in Wilkins book, which strongly suggests to me that years of investigation was carried out by the Police looking at different lines of enquiry.

The author has been trying to figure out what Cooper had in mind when he shouts that the public must hear the evidence before convicting him. Then when convicted at the end of his Trial he shouts that 'evidence' has been withheld. It could be something to do with these cigarette ends. During the trial he may have been waiting for the "cigarette story" to emerge, so that he can say he was not a smoker. On the other hand if his DNA saliva was found on these butt ends, it would have provided strong evidence that it was Cooper watching and observing the front of the Manor prior to the murders.

Consider this. I think Cooper slept rough the night after the murders. It was raining that night and snowing the day after. Even if he had a dry packet of cigarettes on him then he would certainly need another packet a few days later. By the time he returned home he may have heard that the Police were looking for someone that smoked the same cigarettes as him. It was too risky for him to go and buy another packet of twenty, from his usual shop source. This may have inspired the idea that he does not buy any more cigarettes and also the notion that he should give up smoking completely. What a clever deceit.

Brother and sister found shot in blaze home

By JIM SMITH

TWO PEOPLE whose bodies were recovered from their burned-out home in West Wales yesterday died from gunshot wounds, it was revealed last night.

And police admitted later that they could not rule out that it may have been a double murder. Farmer Mr Richard James Thomas, aged 58, and his 51-year-old sister Helen, both unmarried, died in what police have officially described as suspicious circumstances.

The man leading the full-scale inquiry, Detective Chief Superintendent David Davies, head of Dyfed-Powys CID, admitted that it could be murder and a suicide, or double murder. "We have to keep an open mind," he said.

Teams of detectives have been combing the charred ruins of the centuries-old mansion at Scoveston, near Steynton, Milford Haven, for a clue.

But their task was hindered by the severity of the fire which swept through the large home destroying furniture, heirlooms and possible clues to the double tragedy.

Chief inspector John Charles Davies described the deaths of the couple as a mystery. They had lived like recluses, and many officers were carrying out house-to-house inquiries in the immediate area as well as trying to track down relatives.

Mr Thomas's body was found on a half-landing near the first floor by firemen shortly after midnight on Sunday. More than 36 hours later the remains of his sister were discovered amongst charred ruins on the ground floor.

Home Office pathologist, Dr O G Williams carried out post-mortem examinations on both bodies at Withybush Hospital, Haverfordwest, and confirmed that they had died from gunshot wounds.

Firemen were alerted by an off-duty colleague and a motorist, and believe that the blaze, which quickly swept the mansion, had been burning for at least two hours.

The Divisional Commander of Dyfed Fire Service, Mr Ralph Oldacre, of Haverfordwest, said that the fire almost certainly started in one bedroom and quickly spread to the rest of the property.

● The ruins of the mansion where a couple were found dead yesterday.

Western Telegraph cutting. This is the breaking news, regarding Scoveston Manor. The first time the residents of Milford Haven were informed that a double murderer may be at large. The reporter was Jim Smith from Little Haven, an associate of mine who started taking a keen interest, like me, in trying to solve the mystery.

Cortina Car

Amongst the investigation carried out by the Police involved a dark blue Cortina car seen parked at the lay by near the roundabout near the entrance road to Scoveston Manor. Although the Police would have easily traced the car they offered £15,000 pounds reward for information about the owner of the car and why it was parked near the entrance. The car did belong to Cooper who was living close by, but he never came forward to say that the car belonged to him.

Sock from Richard Thomas .

During the intensive search for evidence near Cooper's house in 1998, a sock was found that was assumed to have been taken from Richard Thomas's body when he was murdered. Like the pair of green shorts taken as a trophy from Gwenda Dixon's rucksack, so it looks like Cooper kept a momento of the Scoveston murder by retaining one sock of Richard Thomas. The jury was shown a gruesome photograph of the burnt body of Mr Thomas after the Scoveston fire and the fact that one foot was minus a sock was pointed out to them. DNA testing of the sock showed a match with Richard Thomas. The same sock had fibres from gloves known to be used by Cooper.

Sock from Richard Thomas. It was found near to Cooper's house in Rosemarket. The Forensic Laboratory Service married up fibres from this sock with gloves used by Cooper.
Photograph © Dyfed Powys Police.

At Cooper's trial it was alleged that the glove fibres got onto the sock by the act of Cooper dragging the body of Richard Thomas from the outhouse to the stair landing. However it could also have been "contaminated" by the sock being together with gloves in Cooper's pocket.

Cooper was found guilty of the murder of Richard and Helen Thomas in 2011 and is now serving two life sentences for the crime. Scoveston Manor has been demolished and rebuilt. The house and outbuildings have been converted into Bed & Breakfast and holiday accommodation.

Factors involved in the Scoveston Murders compared to other Cooper crimes .

Two adults killed

A shotgun attack in the front of the house and in the bedroom.

Early evening in the dark, a few days before Christmas.

Someone immensely strong involved

One body moved, dragged and carried after death

Cooper uses diesel to start a fire to destroy vital evidence

No incriminating fingerprints

No obvious motive

Cooper entered knowing a female was alone in the house.

A rural location, surrounded by fields

No shotgun found, no spent cartridges found.

Shotgun stolen from the house a month before.

Cooper may have had keys of the house.

Within a mile of where Cooper was living.

A clothing trophy found near Cooper's house.

Dai Davies, Dyffryn Arms, Gwaun Valley,
Death by a natural stroke?
Date: about 1986
Location: Dyffryn Arms, Gwaun Valley, Pembrokeshire
Who involved: Dai Davies,
Outcome: Not investigated as regarded by all, except the
author, as a natural death .

I used to work with Dai Davies, a supervisor with Pembrokeshire
County Council. He was based at Fishguard and was a long standing
employee of Fishguard and Goodwick Urban District Council. He died
suddenly aged about 60 and no suspicious circumstances were reported
about his death. However I have a strong suspicion that he
could have been another victim of Cooper. Murdered because he
could have known something of Cooper's movements after the
murder of Helen and Richard Thomas. Two days after the Scoveston
Murder (24th December) Dai was driving through Letterston and
picked up a man standing at the crossroads and gave him a lift in a
Council van to Haverfordwest. The same afternoon Dai talked to me
about the man he had picked up and given a lift to, he wanted to tell
me that the man acted in a strange manner. It was a cold wet day and
it had been snowing in Letterston. Dai thought it odd that when the
man got into the passenger seat he kept his hood over his head as
though he was hiding his face from his view. He would not make
conversation except to insist that he was not to be dropped off in
Haverfordwest but that Dai must take a side road before the
town and drop him off near Haverfordwest Railway Station. There
is a bye-pass road now but that had not been completed in 1986. The
man was wearing a green waterproof coat with a large hood, as Dai
explained typical clothing of an agricultural worker. It is not like Dai to
think that anybody was 'odd', which makes his observation more
poignant.
As the Scoveston Murders were the talking point of the day. I told
Dai that he must report the incident to the Police immediately.
The news said the Police were looking for two suspects regarding the
double murder at Scoveston. This was based on the knowledge that Mr
Richards body had been moved quite a distance and carried up some
stairs. On that same day I suggested to Dai that his oddly behaved
passenger could even be one of the two suspected murderers.

The incident was later reported to the Police, but not that day, as Dai was reluctant to do so. Dai did not want to report the incident to the Police as he was not allowed to take passengers, whatever the weather, in his Council van. Dai feared he would be reprimanded by his new boss if he disclosed the story. Also about this time an unoccupied isolated house next to the railway line about two miles south of Fishguard Harbour was broken into through a rear bathroom window. The newspapers reported that someone had eaten tinned food at the house and used the bathroom to have a shave. What is also of interest is that one or two black bicycles were found missing from the house, a most curious theft. The Goodwick residents assumed the burglar to be an Irishman with no money who had come over on the Irish ferry and was making himself comfortable in the first remote and unoccupied house he came across. Unfortunately I have failed to find the exact date this was seen in the newspapers, although with the house being unoccupied for months it could have been months later. If this break in, through a small bathroom window, happened on the night before Dai gave his mystery man a lift, I believe it was Cooper. I have even conjectured that this is where Cooper may have acquired his black bicycle.

Combining the Scoveston incident and the man acting suspiciously at Letterston adds a new dimension to what Cooper may have been doing that Christmas. The likely alibi that Cooper would give his family for not being at home would be that he was busy plucking turkeys, earned so much money that he got drunk and could not return home. Steve Wilkins book mentions that Cooper's daughter told the Police that one evening Cooper came back home with his hair so wet it was flat on his head. As though he had just run home in a panic. He told the family that if anyone asked he was to be at home all evening. Then Cooper went upstairs to shower and change his clothes.

Wilkins surmises that it was the same evening as the Scoveston Murders. If that was the case his daughter would have remembered the date distinctly, but did not want to convey the date to the Police. I think it more likely another occasion, of which there must have been many. Possibly the Mount Estate attack night or after the Sardis attack, when we know that Cooper was seen and he ran straight home in a panic. Originally I thought that Dai's mystery passenger hid his face to hide wounds inflicted at Scoveston. This may have been the case but I now know that Cooper would hide his face with his hood anyway, so that he would not be recognized.

The other factor of significance is that this passenger specifically wished to avoid Haverfordwest town for some reason. Did he think there would be Police or a road block looking for him? Dai would have been going into the centre of Haverfordwest which would have been a short walking distance to the Railway Station anyway. Nevertheless this guy is demanding that he wants to be taken to the train station avoiding the built up area. He knew the road well and knew how to get to the Railway Station, implying he was a local person. I have a strong suspicion that it was Cooper who may have walked all the way up the railway line to Goodwick from Scoveston some 14 miles. For an ordinary man this is a long way to walk. For someone extremely walking fit who is in a panic to get as far away from Scoveston as he could, running for his life, it could be accomplished in 5 hours. Cooper could have broken into the unoccupied house, it is seen from the railway line and is before the urban area of Goodwick. The style of entry is Cooper's and he would have been hungry. The bicycles were unlocked in an outhouse. Cooper on leaving may have taken both, hiding one on the railway line at Dwrbach, Goodwick and using the other to cycle to Letterston. The main road where Dai picked up his passenger is only 6 minutes walk from the disused Letterston railway station. We do not know if Cooper had hidden a bicycle on the track near Scoveston to make this an alternative getaway. However I doubt it but he may have kept a bicycle near the rail station at Johnston. He was now on his way back home via the same route. From Haverfordwest it was an easy walk for Cooper to retrace his steps along the railway line back to Johnson, across a few fields back to his house.

Apart from Letterston being a long way (12 miles) from Milford, I have been thinking why Letterston had an attraction for the Cooper family. His wife moved into a house in Letterston when Cooper was serving time in prison. The same crossroads where Dai picked up his passenger in 1985 is where Cooper was arrested by Police in 2009. Cooper may have had relatives living in a caravan at Trefach. Clunderwen. The biggest attraction may have been the Trecoed Point to Point Horse Races, near Letterston, always attended by Cooper. His wife was very involved with the horses that raced there and she knew many of the Pembrokeshire Hunt members who organised the Point to Point meetings.

It was about a year later that Dai suddenly died. During an evening he went to fetch some wood at an outhouse at the back of the public house in the Gwuan Valley where he lived. He was getting fuel for the lounge fire, but he never came back. Dai was found dead in the yard at the back of the house. It is an area that the customers use to go through to get to the gents urinal. Dai was meant to have died of a stroke. Although Dai was a smoker and a drinker running a pub, he was not overweight and I think he was generally in good health. To me it was a sudden and unexplained death, until I thought of his possible association with Cooper. Cooper was a drinker and a prolific darts player. He would know most of the North Pembrokeshire pubs and would have recognised Dai as living at the pub in the Gwaun Valley pub known as "Bessies ". The Dyffryn Arms is a one room pub like no other. At the time of writing Bessie is aged 87 years old and probably the oldest landlady in Wales. Her pub is also unique and any darts player or drinker living in Pembrokeshire would have visited the pub at least once. The pub is better known for their draughts players than their dart players but it is unique in other ways too. It is one of Pembrokeshire's most famous pubs little changed since 1854 when Bessie's family were first involved. Beer is served in a jug from the barrel. Many people rave about the place because you will find few pubs like it in the world. The last time I visited it was pretty Dickensian with yellow nicotine coloured wallpaper and ten year old cobwebs in the corners. I see by photos on the internet that it has been updated in the last twenty years. Wow, Bessie you are changing with the times! Pontfaen and the Dyffryn Arms celebrate two New Years. The usual one on 1st January (Gregorian Calendar) is a practice for the proper New Year of Hen Galan thirteen days later. This is the New Year in the old Julian Calendar, something they never forget in the Gwaun Valley.

A word of warning. The pub can only be reached by car or horseback. I suggest the latter as the roads around there are extremely icy in the middle of the night on 13th January. A friend of mine skidded his vehicle and killed his passenger when leaving. That is not the recommended way to start a New Year.

Cooper may have had an inkling that Dai had recognised him and could tell the Police of his whereabouts days after the Scoveston murder. If that was the case then Dai would certainly be on Cooper's radar as one who needed to be silenced.

It may be a bit far fetched for me to think that Dai Davies was another victim of Cooper, killed because he was someone who could identify Cooper's movements soon after the Scoveston murders. If the Police had ever questioned Dai about his mystery passenger, and then talked to Cooper about it, Cooper would have known it could only be Dai who had told them. I am pretty confident that Dai's passenger was Cooper, he probably recognized Dai Evans and also knew that he lived at Bessie's pub. I believe there is a good chance that Dai Evans death could have been the hand of Cooper rather than a natural stroke.

Reasons to think Cooper was Dai's mystery passenger.
Man same height as Cooper wearing agricultural clothing.
A green jacket or coat with a large hood.
A local man not wanting his face to be seen.
Someone not wanting to talk.
Someone acting strange and making demands.
Someone not wanting to go into the centre of Haverfordwest yet was seeking a lift in that direction.
A few days after the Scoveston Murders.

Factors involved in a profile of this incident.
(Considered as a natural death it is only the author that has highlighted this sudden death as suspicious.)
One adult known to Cooper, a sudden death.
Happened early evening in the dark.
A rural location, surrounded by fields
Motive, to silence someone who may have recognized Cooper and his movements.

Florence Evans. Suspicious Death.
Date: 4th February 1989, body discovered 5th Feb 1989.
Location: Thornhill, Rosemarket, Pembrokeshire.
Outcome: "Accidental Death" verdict by Coroner Howells.

74 year old (sometimes reported as 73 years old) Florence "Flo" Evans was a very independent woman and a retired farmer. Since her husband had died, a few years before, she lived by herself in a house in Rosemarket. She was friendly with Cooper who did odd jobs for her. On 5th February 1989 she was found dead in her bath in her house. The Coroner decided the cause of death was that she had fallen into the bath and struck her head and died. Her immediate friends thought otherwise for a number of reasons and openly said so at the time. They suspected foul play by another party. Everyone thought it was more than odd that a healthy and fit pensioner should die after falling into her bath. It was reported by the newspaper and to the Coroner that she was found fully clothed with her head downwards in a half filled bath.

During 2011 one of the newspapers reported that this death had happened a few months after the Dixon Murders. Flo Evans death was actually five months before the Dixon tragedy. The inquest of her death was in April 1989. This is only about 5 or 6 weeks before Cooper goes to the ITV Studios on 30 May to be filmed for the Bullseye Show which was televised on 22 June 1989.

Cooper himself said at his 2011 Trial that "Flo and her husband Archie were the first to welcome us [Cooper and his late seamstress wife Pat] into Rosemarket when we moved there." When I read this my immediate reaction was, what happened to Archie? What were the circumstances of his death? How many months before Flo's death did Archie die ? and were there any suspicious circumstances that could be attributed to Cooper involvement ? The author has read that there were no suspicious circumstances about his death, but who is giving this opinion? Even when sudden deaths and suspicious ones are investigated the Coroner has made some dubious and controversial conclusions.

The house named Thornhill where Flo Evans died has now been demolished. It was located on the northern edge of Rosemarket and had fields adjacent to it. As the house has now gone it is unlikely that any new evidence from the area will shed any new light on her death. As her death was determined "Accidental" it is now unlikely to be changed to a murder enquiry. Flo lived by herself in the house and those that knew her said that she never had a bath there. If hot water was needed in a bath it was via a back boiler in the living room fireplace. No fire had been lit in this fireplace to provide hot water for the bath. It was the coldest month and if Flo was going to have a bath she would have prepared the fire to get the hot water ready. This was not done. The Coroner was told that she was found fully clothed in a bath half full of cold water, and still wearing her slippers. She had a small wound to her head. A bizarre situation indeed and one that looks more like a murder scene than an unfortunate accident of a once very active pensioner. I have since talked to someone who worked in Rosemarket at the time, who made the comment "Flo was found completely naked wearing Wellington boots upside down in a cold bath that she never used and the Coroner thinks there were no suspicious circumstances!" I was instantly intrigued at this contrary description of what Flo was wearing. The information had come from a close neighbour of Flo's, who also had a key to her front door. Suspecting something not quite right he had tried opening the front door with his key and found that the deadlock on the lock had been activated, something Flo never did. That morning her niece had gone shopping with Flo Evans. When the death was realized that same person knew that there were unusual things about the house. First of all the bath was never used and was now half filled with water. The television had been turned off using the on/off dial switch yet Flo always disconnected it at the plug which had not been done in this case. She also mentioned that the cats were inside the house, an odd fact to her. Her family also reported that her purse was missing. When questioned by Coroner Howells, Flo's aunt had to admit that she could not see any evidence of an attack. There was a cut in the linoleum near to the bath and a slipped mat suggesting that Flo Evans could have slipped and fallen face down into the bath.

Detective Inspector Tom Peter explained to the Coroner that the deadlock on both front and back porch doors must have been engaged from the inside and there were no signs of forced or attempted forced entry. To say this with certainty he must have interviewed the neighbour who broke into the house through the porch window and opened the locked front door. One of the people who first found Flo, not only says that she was naked except for her wellies (Wellington boots) but that one arm was behind her back, as though someone had held her upside down in a Half Nelson grip to drown her. These facts were never revealed to the Coroner. The same neighbour knew that Pat Cooper had a front door key as she sometimes cleaned for Flo. Cooper would have known of this. It would seem that Cooper did put deadlocks on the doors from inside yet left via a porch window that could be shut from outside.

Cooper was familiar with the house, its layout and windows. About one week before she died Flo had mentioned to friends that her house keys had gone missing. From our knowledge of how Cooper operated, we now know that it was probably Cooper who had stolen them. If he already knew his wife had a key this is an extremely cunning plot as to not implicate his wife in a planned murder. The reason that the Pembrokeshire Coroner Mr Michael Howell recorded a verdict of accidental death, was all due to the locks on the doors being found secure. Also that no evidence of foul play was discovered. He said the fact that the deadlocks to both doors to the house were locked from the inside indicated there could not have been an intruder. Cooper was not only an expert at entering houses he would certainly be familiar with leaving a property fully locked up. The Coroner had not contemplated the fact that the intruder may have taken the keys the week before and locked the doors on leaving. I now know that both Pat Cooper and another neighbour both had a key to Flo's house, deliberately passed to them by Flo herself in case they needed to look after the house if she was not there. The black bicycle, so prominent with the description of the man collecting money with Dixon's bank card, remained leaning against the back wall of Flo's house during the whole time of her death Inquest. It was still there months later when her house was up for sale, when the Police were looking for the Dixon murderer.

The more consideration that is put into the situation, it is more than likely Cooper visited Flo Evans's house that evening with the intention to kill her. If he already had keys to the house he could have committed a burglary when she was out of the house earlier that day. He would have known that during the week she often had her niece staying with her. If he was going to carry out a murder at Thornhill, it would have to be at the weekend. Flo was found dead on the only night of the week when she was alone. Cooper would know exactly if Flo was at home and if she had company or not. Even if Cooper was dressed in his customary dark balaclava. or not, Flo would have recognised Cooper. No evidence was seen in the house or on Flo's body of extreme violence. But if they both knew each other and it had been well preplanned, that is expected. Cooper probably only had one thing on his mind and that was of killing Florence to silence her. He may not have had his shotgun with him at the time, and he may not have needed his balaclava. He has had enough time to think of a plan and filling the bath with water and making her death look like an accident must have come to him as the best idea. In retrospect it was cunning as it fooled both the Police and the Coroner, but not the Rosemarket residents.

We will never know what happened inside the house of Flo Evans on the day she died, but there seems to be an overwhelming certainty that Cooper was involved. Another likely scenario is that Cooper was having a friendly chat that day with Flo Evans in her house, or visiting to collect some of her home made brew, and something in the conversation (perhaps a mention of the Scoverston murders) triggered Cooper's killer instinct to silence her. Richard Thomas of Scoveston was also known to collect home made wine and beer from Flo Evans. It must be said that others in Rosemarket who knew both Cooper and Flo, would have suspected Cooper as the murderer of Flo. However being neighbours they would never publicly suggest names, or point a finger for fear of their own lives and because of their close relationship with Pat Cooper. This secrecy of being too scared to inform the Police of Cooper's association with Flo resulted in Cooper managing to continue his murderous ways.

Mrs Evans' niece Jean Murphy had seen Flo the morning she died. She was one who had mentioned to Police that there were a lot of things that were not usual when her aunt's body was found. Like some of Cooper's other suspected crimes, the Police did not appear to pursue the most obvious line of investigation and once the Coroner's verdict was given any murder inquiry was immediately halted. Here, once again, it would seem the Police did not do enough talking to the neighbours. For instance, I have learnt that the neighbour opposite noticed that the upstairs curtains had been closed on the night Flo died. The neighbour said that Flo usually kept those curtains open and it was unusual to see them closed. This fact was never recorded by the Police because they did not interview this neighbour, the closest. before the Inquest.

Did this once again allow Cooper to get away with murder? I think the answer is an emphatic, Yes! It extended Cooper's evasion of capture and increase his confidence that he could do it again. It is becoming a hobby. It is this crime that I believe initiated his odd statement of having an 'Unusual Hobby'.

His application to be a Game Show contestant was posted to the ITV studios about the same time as Flo's death. A post mortem examination revealed a minor laceration to Flo's forehead but there were no marks of violence. Cause of death was given as drowning and it was suggested she could well have tripped and fallen into the bath or may have suddenly collapsed. The injury to the forehead, the Pathologist's said, could have rendered Flo Evans unconscious. The Coroner said *"there were one or two features of the case that caused disquiet to the family and obviously matters to be investigated. However Mrs Evans' position in the bath indicated clearly she had fallen and was not placed there. The alternative was to assume someone ran the bath and waited for her there, hit her on the head, pushed her into the bath and escaped through a door which was locked from the inside."*

I don't think from the evidence that can be supported," Coroner Howells told the inquest, recording a verdict of Accidental Death. By recording this verdict, no further investigation is going to be made, so why did the Coroner mention "obvious matters to be investigated"? He could have delayed his verdict until these things had been investigated. The alternative theory he gave seems to be exactly what happened, which now seems obvious to everybody concerned.

The Coroner's assumption that Mrs Evans' position in the bath indicates she had fallen and was not placed there, I am sure, was an incorrect assumption. The Coroner did not have the additional information that one of her arms was behind her back, in the exact position it would be if someone was holding her down in a Half-Nelson arm lock while she was drowned. The Policeman who wrote his report on what he saw may have failed to add this bit to his report thinking a face down position seemed a sufficient description. The Policeman may have thought it was an intruder drowning Flo Evans but had not emphasised that fact to the Coroner. When the Coroner had made his judgement the Policeman must have remained silent, embarrassed that it was his report that lacked some vital details.

We know that Cooper was immensely strong and could lift anyone directly into a bath, especially an elderly woman half his weight. We also know that if he had done so he would have positioned the body so that it looked like an accident, so that it would confuse detectives. If somebody is falling into a bath both their arms would go forward to arrest the fall. Cooper knew the house and knew Flo Evans, and we can assume that he had spent considerable time in planning such a murder. He was probably the one holding her house keys and could lock the doors in such a manner that it looked like they were locked from inside, or could escape through a window that automatically closed behind him.

What Cooper did not know was that Flo Evans never filled the bath, and certainly would not do so without starting the fire and back boiler in the living room to warm the water up first. If Cooper had known this, he could easily have started a fire there to add to the deception. If he had closed the upper room curtains he could have opened them up again, but then he may have been seen from across the road. After the guilty verdict of four murders for Cooper in 2011, The Western Telegraph newspaper contacted Jean Murphy who said "We had suspicions about her death at the time, and still want answers so we can draw a line under it all.

It was a shock when she died. I saw her earlier that day. Some things just weren't right. We couldn't find her purse and the bath was cold, and the cats were in. "There are lots of unanswered questions." Mrs Murphy's daughter Julie added: "There were some funny things about the house at the time. We're not getting our hopes up, we may never know what happened to her." There was some genuine hope of answers soon after the Cooper trial in 2011, but now, at the time of writing, some six years later, Julie's realistic view is the more likely. The Public Prosecution Service seem to have no intention of a review, to overturn the dubious Coroner's decision, and to start a murder enquiry. All the evidence suggests that Flo was murdered by Cooper, what is significant is that Cooper had adopted a different murder method.

This is the time for Cooper to confess, something he is unlikely to do. It would make no difference to his being in jail, but would be an honourable gesture to the community in which he was a part. If the public and residents now accept that Flo Evans was another of Cooper's victims, there is perhaps no need for more public money to be spent on another County Court Trial and the truth being recorded.

Factors involved in a profile of this incident. (Not yet regarded by the Police as a murder)
One adult known to Cooper suddenly dies.
Carried out early evening in the dark.
Someone extremely strong involved.
Pets inside. Some cash stolen.
Motive: to silence someone who suspected Cooper's crimes.
Deceased found naked, in a position as though being held underwater
House locked up.
Rural location, house surrounded by fields.
Cooper thought to have keys to the house.
When her husband died, shotguns went missing.

"Artie" Archie Evans of Thornhill, Rosemarket.
Recorded as a Natural death about 1987
Outcome: Only the author considers he may be a Cooper victim.

I would like to know more about the circumstances of Flo's husband's death. Artie /Archie died about two years before Flo. He had some shotguns that disappeared after his death. Apart from running a smallholding he was a Point to Point jockey, Cooper knew him well and would have placed bets on him to win at such events. One of the main Point to Point meetings in Pembrokeshire was at Trecoed, near Letterston. There was a great friendship between Archie, his wife Flo and Cooper. Being much younger, fitter and more able and living only a short distance away, Cooper was very useful to Archie and Flo. What must have maintained this relationship was that Flo made homemade brew and Cooper liked his beer. Cooper helped them with outdoor jobs and collecting winter feed for their livestock. On at least one occasion he collected bales of hay from Scoveston Manor in a vehicle and delivered it to Flo's smallholding. Being so close to Cooper, and also having visited Scoveston the couple may have suspected that Cooper was responsible for the murder of Richard and Helen Thomas and the burning down of Scoveston Manor.

Fearing any reprisal from Cooper they would have kept their silence and not mentioned their suspicion to anyone. Archie died suddenly within a year and a half after the Scoveston Murders. I have a suspicion that he may have been murdered by Cooper. History shows that Cooper would not hesitate to commit murder on anyone that he thought may know of his crimes or could identify him to the Police. As the Thomas family was an integral part of the Rosemarket community the subject of the Scoveston Murders must have arisen in idle conversation between Archie and Cooper. If Cooper suspected that Archie knew too much about his 'unusual hobbies' it would have spelt the death sentence for Archie.

If Archie did not suspect Cooper as a killer, he would undoubtedly have talked to Cooper about the murders. Being reminded about them may have provoked Cooper into killing him. I have failed to find the circumstances of Archie's death but the Police and Coroner considered there were no unusual circumstances. Knowing what we now know about Cooper, and his involvement with this couple, Archie's death should also be investigated as a Cooper victim.

For an astute serial killer like Cooper, finding a method to kill Archie over a period of one year, to make it look "natural" is a relatively easy task. We know that Cooper can get aggressively violent and vindictive when provoked and also that he silences people who know too much about his "unusual hobby". Was Archie Evans another of Cooper's victims? It was about two years later when Flo Evans mysteriously died. The local people thought Cooper had a key to their house. Flo Evans, may also have provoked Cooper by talking about the Scoveston Murders, but it is more likely she knew Cooper was the prime suspect yet was too scared to tell anybody of her fears. I strongly believe that many of the residents of Rosemarket suspected Cooper was involved with the Scoveston murders yet kept their mouths shut to the Police, terrified to be the first one that would point the finger at Cooper. They still kept their silence when Flo Evans was murdered, expecting the Police to find the culprit rather than to suggest it was one of their community. In July 2008 when Cooper was nearing the end of his prison term for previous burglaries and armed attack, he was extensively interviewed by the Police. During this interview Cooper admitted his friendship with Flo Evans. The Police then, could have sought a review of the Coroner's decision on Flo's death to start another murder enquiry. To the general public Cooper's connectivity with Flo Evan's did not reveal itself until his Swansea Trial in 2011. Obviously the Police did not seek a Coroner's review on Flo's death in 2008 for fear that it would jeopardize or divert their investigation into Cooper. It took another three years for Steve Wilkins and his team to collect the evidence for the Scoveston and Dixon Murders. I maintain if they had also charged Cooper with Flo's death then it would have aided rather than hindered the prosecution of the other crimes. To review a Coroner's verdict and admit to the public that the Police did not investigate a murder competently, is such a big deal that it just does not happen in Wales. The Police think it undermines the public perception of them and the Justice system. Of course it does, but it also perpetuates Injustice in the British Judicial system which is far more important than the esteem of any Police Force.

The Dixon Murders
Date: Thursday 29 June 1989
Location: on the cliff path near Little Haven, Pembrokeshire
Who involved : Peter Dixon and his wife Gwenda Dixon
Outcome: Cooper found Guilty of Murder, sentenced to two life
terms of imprisonment in 2011.

Peter and Gwenda Dixon enjoyed the outdoor life. Pembrokeshire to them was a second home, a welcome break from the hustle and bustle of city life near London. They enjoyed the coastline so much that every year for 15 years they would visit Pembrokeshire for their summer holidays. They had been married for 27 years and for this holiday in June they decided to camp, with a small zip up two man tent. Using the tent suited their healthy lifestyle and meant not having to bother with any prior booking for holiday accommodation. They picked Howelston Camping and Caravan site to pitch their tent. It was close to Little Haven and only a field away from the Pembrokeshire Coast Path with its stunning sea cliff scenery. As it was the last day of a ten day holiday, Peter and Gwenda Dixon decided to go for a morning walk before setting off in the late morning to drive back to their home at Witney in Oxfordshire, about a four hour drive. They were camping in a small pea-green tent which was still wet with the morning dew. Zipping the tent up, allowing the sun to dry it and locking their Ford Sierra car they set off for a walk along the coast path. Peter Dixon (51 years old) having binoculars slung around his neck and a camera while Gwenda (52 years old) carried a small rucksack on her back. They crossed the large fields and headed for the cliff path. It was a walk they had done scores of times and never tired of it. They intended returning to the camp site an hour or so later giving them plenty of time to return home to suburbia that afternoon. The day was Thursday 29th June 1989 and the time was 9.30 am. It was a fine midsummer morning. The couple were seen leaving the caravan site, but they never returned.

Within the next 45 minutes the couple had been tied up, brutally shot at point blank range and their blood soaked bodies carefully hidden in undergrowth. Despite the murder inquiry being one of the biggest ever conducted in the United Kingdom, Cooper evaded capture until 2011. As John Cooper has never admitted involvement in any of his crimes, we are never likely to know exactly what happened on the cliff path that morning. The most likely scenario is that Cooper was in hiding waiting for someone to rob, kill or sexually assault. It seems a most odd place to rob anyone as most walking the path are only likely to have the bare minimum of cash on them, perhaps enough to buy a midday meal at a public house or cafe. To have a sexual motive one would think he could have waited for a younger single girl or a group of women. Had he waited longer there would have been such a group as the Pembrokeshire Coast Path is an extremely popular walk, especially in June, with people of all descriptions and nationalities partaking of one of the best cliff walks in the world.

One can conclude that Cooper had murder on his mind; to kill any couple, and also take their bank cards. Cooper may have decided to target the first man and wife couple that he saw. An older couple the better as they are likely to have a healthier bank account, and possibly carrying more than one Bank card with them. His intention may have been to kill any couple, having killed a couple before and got away with it, he may have had a thirst to carry out another double killing. He had done it before, can he do it again and evade capture? In Cooper's mind his television appearance was a public humiliation. In fact not winning anything in the Bullseye Show meant to Cooper that he was a loser, and worse still he had done it in front of millions of viewers. This was now his big chance to prove to himself that he was not a failure, to prove he still had his touch for his unusual hobby, of killing again and avoiding detection.

Cooper lay in hiding at the side of the cliff path, dressed in his customary long coat, balaclava and gloves with shotgun already loaded, he was ready to pounce. At just the correct moment to cause maximum shock Cooper jumps in front of the Dixon's and shouting like a maniac commands them to stop. In a spate of premeditated violence he leads them at gunpoint just off the public path to where he wants them, on lower more densely covered ground. He ties the hands of Peter Dixon behind his back, and does the same to Gwenda. The Dixons are both aware that there is little they can do to resist or attempt to fight off this madman. Cooper used two pieces of polypropylene cord to tie their hands behind their backs. He had brought the cord with him, specially for the purpose. Cooper demands money and takes the wallet belonging to Peter. Cooper then gets the couple to kneel on the ground and interrogates them in a terrifying ordeal until they reveal the correct PIN number for Peter Dixon's National Westminster bank card. This is happening on a flattish plateaux of land only 18 meters from the cliff path. It is a small copse completely hidden from the coastal path, a spot preplanned by Cooper, who had spent time picking the correct location for his actions and an execution. In order to obtain the card PIN number or as an act of venting his brutal aggression Cooper strikes a wounding blow to the head of Gwenda. After obtaining the correct PIN number the couple were both shot dead at close range with a shotgun. Gwenda Dixon suffered a shotgun wound in her back and her right chest and a wounding blow to the head. Peter Dixon was shot three times, one in the face, one in the back and in the right chest, his hands still tied behind his back. The lower clothing of Mrs Dixon, her shorts and panties were missing. It is not known if Cooper removed these before or after she had been shot. The Pathologist report stated that there was actually no evidence of a sexual assault on her although it is thought her bra had been displaced before she was shot. Cooper was to take the shorts from the scene and keep them for himself.

Cooper removed the wedding ring from the finger of Mr Dixon, but did not take either of their wrist watches, the binoculars or the camera. The individual reselling values of these would have been much more than the wedding ring, but of course, more identifiable to the crime.

Cooper then proceeded to hide the two blood soaked bodies. He lifted the body of Peter Dixon and carried it to the cliff edge, a matter of about 6 meters, with the intention of throwing it down the steep and rocky cliff. The body did not fall over the cliff as intended but remained very close to the top, so close that it was dangerous for Cooper to repeat the manoeuvre with Gwenda's body. The position of Peter's body was found on a sloping piece of ground already ten meters below the top of the cliff edge, with a sheer 70 meter (230 foot) drop below. The position was so precarious that the Policeman who recovered the body did so with the help of the Coastguard Cliff Rescue Team. Cooper was forced into plan B, that of hiding the bodies with undergrowth, as he had learnt with his survival skills and read about in his Survival Manual. Collecting foliage and digging up bracken with their roots, using his commando knife, he carefully replanted them around the body of Peter Dixon . When hidden from view, he repeated the process around the body of Gwenda. Her body was positioned next to hazel trees and the pliable branches carefully intertwined to make a screen. The vegetation was matted and intertwined with living branches making a dense screen to hide each body. So effective was each covering that even close up it was almost impossible to see a body beneath. Cooper kept his woollen gloves on to break branches and twigs. Later detectives found glove fibres on the broken branches. Thrown over the cliff were discarded items and the Dixon's small rucksack that looked that it had been rifled for anything of value. Cooper may have hoped to find another wallet in the rucksack. A pair of shorts, so crucial for evidence, was thought to have been taken from the rucksack and worn by Cooper later that day. Peter Dixon's wallet, minus his National Westminster bank card, was found nearby.

Picture of the murder scene 70 meters above the sea, Little Haven
village is in the distance. After shooting Gwenda Dixon twice and
Peter Dixon three times, Cooper attempted to throw their bodies
over the cliff. It was one of the most brutal murders Wales has
ever witnessed. If you visit the location today there is a small
slate memorial tablet marking the spot that is pinned to a tree.
Photographed by the author in 2014.

The Murder Scene

The location for the murder had been carefully chosen by Cooper . It was a remote part of the Pembrokeshire Coast Path yet easily accessed from the coast road. Leaving a vehicle on the coast road it takes only five minutes to walk across two fields to get to the murder scene. It would take twice that time to walk down the coast path from Howelston Caravan Site where the Dixons were staying. Although Cooper knew Howelston Camp site well it is thought he had not stalked the Dixon's or knew them in any way. Cooper lay in wait for the first couple to come down the footpath. The single file footpath is on the seaward side of a high earthen bank. It is in a natural dip in the landscape and even someone in the fields above would not be able to see what was going on in the coast path below, just a few yards away, because their view is blocked by an earthen bank and a hedgerow. There is a direct view up and down the path at the point of ambush; Cooper can easily see if anyone else is coming along the lane, making sure nobody else can interfere with his planned attack. On the seaward side of the path is a thicket of hazel and stunted oak trees and a natural copse or dell less than twenty meters from the path. It is here that the Dixons were murdered. Today the site has a small commemorative plaque, an inscribed slate positioned on the trunk of a tree.

In his initial interviews, Cooper denied to the Police that he ever went near to Little Haven . He was known to work for a time with the National Trust. The National Trust manage land near to the cliff path at Kete, Dale, and at Porth y Rhaw, Solva only seven miles away from Little Haven. Later in one of his interviews Cooper told Police he launched small boats from the slipway at both Broad Haven and Little Haven and had sold mackerel in the villages. Cooper's son, once used his father's car to visit the area of Little Haven after the murders. Cooper when he knew, was absolutely furious with his son, using the excuse that one of the tyres was bald and he could be prosecuted. Adrian added the information that his father knew he used the car but only went berserk when Little Haven had been mentioned. It pointed to a suspicion of guilt with his father over the murders.

Although the location of the killings may seem somewhat odd, to Cooper it had been preplanned. His wife, Patricia, was known to visit the same caravan site, she helped clean and tidy up some of the caravans on a weekly basis and also made and fitted cushions, curtains and furnishings for some of the caravan owners. Cooper used to drive her over to the Howelston Caravan Site on the mornings she was employed as a cleaner and dropped her off. Cooper would not be one to hang around waiting for his wife, so, on some occasions, he is likely to have gone for an hour's walk. He would have walked to the cliff path, exactly the same route taken by the Dixon's some time later. It may have been on one of these walks that Cooper realized it was an ideal spot for him to commit his next double murder. The author does not know if Cooper drove to Little Haven on the day of the murder or that his wife was with him that day. If Pat habitually got caravans ready for weekend holiday makers, then a Thursday and Friday may have been her busy days at Howelston. Cooper may have driven her there and she had an arrangement to return home on the afternoon bus. I do not know the exact dates but Cooper was known to use a bicycle around this time as he was banned from driving his car for a year. It must have been during this time that his son Adrian was making use of his father's car. Could Adrian have driven his mother to Howelston on that fateful day? We do not know and certainly it is not information known to the Police, as they seemed to be totally unaware of Pat Cooper's movements on the day in question. It is quite feasible that after the murder Cooper walked back to the caravan site, got into his car and drove home. When home he changes into shorts, washes and hides his shotgun, locks his gloves in his outhouse and picks up his bicycle. As quickly as possible he cycles over the Cleddau Bridge towards Pembroke where he intends to do two actions. One is to extract money from Peter Dixon's bank card, the pin number securely written down on a note in his pocket. The second thing is to get some money from the Pembroke Jeweller for Peter's wedding ring also in his shorts pocket.

Three hours after the killings Cooper is seen with his bicycle in Pembroke. Those noticing him have no idea that he has committed a double murder, but one witness gives evidence that he looked very suspicious. Cooper is dressed for cycling without his long jacket, shotgun, etc. We know that Cooper has taken these somewhere, and the most obvious place is to his house which is en route between Little Haven and the Cleddau Bridge. Gwenda Dixon was wearing long trousers when murdered and her son said that she would have taken shorts in her rucksack for wearing if it became hot. It is these very shorts that Cooper not only took as a trophy but changed into for his bike ride to Pembroke. The artist impression of Cooper distributed to the public not only was accurate in his hairstyle but also in showing him wearing Gwenda Dixon's shorts. These shorts were later shortened by Cooper's seamstress wife Pat to be less identifiable.

Cash Point ATM withdrawals
On the day of the killings and about 20 miles south of Little Haven, Cooper, described as a scruffy haired man with a bicycle, was seen twice near the Bank Cash point (Lloyds Bank) in Pembroke High Street. The time of one sighting was about 1.30 pm and the other sighting about 4 pm at the same place. One witness was working in a bakery opposite the Lloyds Bank in Pembroke and watched a man acting suspiciously. She told the jury she recalled seeing a man standing outside the Bank for between 15 and 20 minutes. She said he was dressed in shorts or cut-off trousers, had scruffy grey collar length hair and an "old fashioned" straight handle bar bike. "There was something unusual about him. When I would look at him he would look away," she said. Other witnesses in Pembroke described the same man who had a "weather beaten face". This is not surprising as Cooper was naturally swarthy looking but also had just ridden his bicycle over the Cleddau Bridge, about ten miles, on a hot sunny day. Two withdrawal extractions were made with the card that afternoon in Pembroke, the total amount extracted being £110 pounds.

It is feasible that one of the reasons that Cooper chose Pembroke ATM is that he had Peter Dixon's wedding ring with him and wanted to cash it in with Pembroke Jeweller Ray Smith. The jeweller's shop is only a few shops away from the Cash Point on the same street. It was a shop familiar to Cooper as he had cashed in stolen goods at this shop before. This time he wanted to make a deal on the Dixon ring as soon as possible, before the dead bodies were discovered. It could be that Cooper went to the shop before going to the Cash point ATM (about 1.30 pm) but found Ray Smith not there, or was told he had not returned from lunch. Frustrated and agitated Cooper may have been looking up and down the street looking for Ray Smith to return to his shop. This may account for the witness seeing Cooper looking suspicious.

Over the next three days Cooper extracted a total amount of £310 from four withdrawals. The extracted amounts were in groups of £10 or £100. Two days later Cooper made a withdrawal at Haverfordwest National Westminster Bank. This withdrawal was the last one made and probably coincided with Cooper realizing that the Police knew that a card used was from the missing person Peter Dixon.

Additional money was added to the Peter Dixon's bank account by the Police, in the hope that more withdrawals would be made. Withdrawals stopped three days after the murders, which was three days before the bodies were found. When extracting money from an ATM machine, a witness would not notice or know if someone was illegally extracting. However if this act combined with Cooper actually waiting or looking out for someone who may know him, would make anyone, even a man like Cooper, look suspicious. Cooper failed to meet up with Ray Smith the jeweller that afternoon, so he kept the ring in his pocket. It was six days later that Cooper returned to the Pembroke Jeweller's shop, saw Ray Smith and sold the ring to him.

The Cleddau Bridge had video cameras but the recordings were not kept long enough to be of use in the investigation. The next day (30th May) Cooper went to Carmarthen and also made a successful ATM Cash Point withdrawal using Peter Dixon's card. The very next morning Nicholas Elliott, who had heard through Police friends about the "weather beaten man with the bicycle", was specifically looking for such a man when he spotted him. Mr Elliot was driving through Haverfordwest on his way to work, when he saw the man he knew the Police were looking for. One has to ask the question why the local Police were not watching the nearest National Westminster Cash point to where they knew the Dixon's card was likely stolen? Mr Elliott's wife actually worked at the same bank and so he carefully made a note of what he was seeing. He told Police that he saw a man making a cash withdrawal at 7.14 am in Haverfordwest on July 1, 1989 (ie two days after Cooper had been seen in Pembroke.) he was standing next to a black bicycle with straight handle-bars, and was described as the outdoor type. If the Police had acted quickly then and cordoned Haverfordwest off, the man on the bicycle would have been apprehended. However the Dixon bodies had not been discovered and the Police did not know that this man was a murder suspect at this time. The Dixon's were still two missing people at this stage. From Mr Elliott's description and that of witnesses in Pembroke a second artist's impression drawing was made and circulated. This drawing was not issued to the public until 9th July, after the Police knew it was a murder enquiry. In retrospect, although it is an excellent artist's impression, this image over the next year actually hindered rather than helped the investigation. On the three days following the killings, Cooper collected cash from various ATM machines using the Dixon's National Westminster Cash Card. Only one of the relevant ATM machines had a CCTV camera mounted near it. Unfortunately this one did not have any recording for the Police to look at. The Bank ATM machines that were visited by Cooper included National Westminster Bank in Haverfordwest High Street, one in the middle of Carmarthen, and the Lloyds Bank in Pembroke High Street.

Once the Police had commenced their murder investigation they notified the public that Mr Dixon's Cash Card had been stolen and alerted people to look out for a wild looking man with a bicycle that had been seen near some of the banks. An artist's impression made up from witnesses in Pembroke and Haverfordwest of the suspicious character was circulated on 9th July via the Television news and the newspapers. This Press Release was made ten days after the first sighting outside a bank in Pembroke High Street.

On the morning of the murders, shots of gunfire were heard in the locality at about 10.30 am. A man cutting grass at All Saints Church down the hill at Little Haven thought he heard shots at that time. Also holidaymakers on Little Haven beach, more than a mile away, heard some bangs but being an agricultural area, such sounds were not unusual. Especially as it was common to have explosive bird scares making bangs in the fields where barley was being grown. Nobody saw Cooper at the scene of the murders and it was many days before it was realized that Peter and Gwenda Dixon had gone missing. Two different close friends of mine were within a mile of the scene when it happened but neither could shed any light on the investigation when questioned by the Police.

Hiding the bodies carefully in the undergrowth and the fact that the Dixon's were not missed for four days allowed Cooper to get away from the Police. That delay made the investigation a hundred times more difficult. It was the start of the working week when Tim Dixon, in Oxfordshire, realized that his parents had not returned home from their West Wales holiday.

The Dixon Family.
Peter Dixon, aged 51, was a marketing consultant in Oxfordshire, and his work took him around the London area. Gwenda, was aged 52, and worked as a secretary with the Social Services Department in the same area. Peter Dixon worked a hectic life in London and he regarded walking in Pembrokeshire as his annual antidote and relaxation. He was also known to go jogging and generally kept himself fit.

83

Gwenda, likewise, kept herself fit by playing Badminton and was a Committee member at the local Badminton Club. They were a well liked, joyful couple, who contributed much to the town of Witney where they lived. They had a daughter, Julie, aged 19 and a son, Tim, aged 23. The same weekend as Mr and Mrs Dixon went missing, Julie, their daughter, was returning from her short Cyprus summer holiday. She tried telephoning the home of her parents and was perplexed at getting no answer from the family house. Together, with her brother Tim, they drove over to their parent's house and discovered that their parents had not returned home from their Pembrokeshire holiday. It was the start of the working week and Peter Dixon had not turned up at his workplace. Tim Dixon telephoned the Howelston Camp Site, who told them that the car and tent were still there but they had not seen Peter or Gwenda for a few days. It was only then that the Police were alerted that the couple were missing. This was four days after the murders and at the beginning it was not a murder inquiry; the Police and family were looking for two missing adults.

Tim Dixon drove down to Little Haven to help with the search of his parents. During the previous week he had actually visited them for the day in Pembrokeshire and nothing had seemed out of place when he had last seen them. A search was made of the area using the Police, Police dog handlers and the public. Two days later a volunteer noticed an area near the cliff top that had a lot of flies and a pungent smell. He alerted one of the Police Dog Handlers to the spot and the body of Gwenda was first discovered covered under foliage and then the body of Peter Dixon further over the cliff. The Pathologist was notified and Home Office Pathologist Professor . Bernard Knight, arrived on the scene later that same day. When leading Pathologist Bernard Knight studied the shotgun wounds he told the Police that they showed precision and were the work of someone familiar with firing shotguns. He confirmed that the Police were now looking for a double murderer.

As Cooper was seen in Pembroke three and a half hours after committing the murders, then he would undoubtedly have crossed the Cleddau Bridge with his bicycle. There is an alternative route from Little Haven to Pembroke avoiding the Cleddau Bridge but it would take twice as long to get there. The Cleddau Bridge at the time had CCTV cameras on it and would have have made a video of Cooper going across it. No mention of rerunning the Cleddau Bridge CCTV videos to look for a cyclist, was seen by the author in the newspaper articles at the time. It may have been the fact that the Cleddau Bridge video recordings were only kept for about five days at that time and it was at least six days of past recordings that were relevant. In later years the author has studied CCTV footage taken on the Cleddau Bridge to identify vehicles under an entirely different investigation. If such footage was available for the police in the Dixon Murders, it is quite possible Cooper would have been apprehended decades earlier for this crime. Also the same would apply if CCTV monitor cameras were sited at all the bank ATM outlets, as they are today.

It is often said in Murder Investigations that if the murderer is not apprehended in six weeks then there is a good probability it will remain an unsolved crime.

No connectivity of Cooper or his wife to Howelston Camp Site was ever mentioned in the Swansea Trial, which makes one wonder if the investigating Police knew about Pat being a cleaning helper at the site. As far as I am aware Pat Cooper was not formally questioned about the murders once in the entire investigation. The Police had her husband as the prime suspect for the two double murders from 1995 and yet still in 2005 evidence from Cooper alone was still being collected. Cooper's Trial was in 2011 and yet in all that time Pat Cooper was not interviewed properly by the Police. One has to ask the question, Why not? I can only think of two likely reasons why she was not investigated. One because the Police knew her and her influential friends too well and did not want to implicate her. Alternatively the Police, for some obtuse reason did not want Cooper, who was in prison for most of the time, to realize that the Police were investigating him.

Pat Cooper from day one could have told the Police about her connectivity with Howelston Campsite and how her husband knew Flo Evans and the Richards at Scoveston. She was never formally questioned and given the opportunity to do so and thus extended the investigation for a further ten years and, I maintain, cost her her life as well.

Shotguns discovered but not investigated.

A tradesman who worked in the Little Haven area told me that one day someone noticed that a shotgun had been discarded in a black bag near the St Bride's Haven telephone box. This is less than two miles from the murder scene. The Police were notified but even according to Steve Wilkins's book, the Police did not spend any time investigating who it belonged to. Additionally another shotgun and ammunition belt was discovered in a hedge at Freystrop some weeks after Cooper's Mount Estate teenager attack incident, only a mile away, also unidentified. I consider it most odd if the Police did not do additional investigations into the gun left by the roadside in St Bride's especially as they are investigating a double shotgun murder in the same area. Did the Police think that the murderer or a hoaxer deliberately planted these as a decoy to implicate someone else?

Because the style of the Dixon killings was so brutal and looked like an execution after an interrogation it was thought that there may be an association with an IRA drugs or arms smuggling operation. One theory being that the Dixon couple while watching peregrine falcons on the coast path had actually seen IRA men hiding a cache of guns and were killed by terrorists who wished to silence them. This notion gained more support when an IRA cache was found some years later between Little Haven and Newgale.

The Dixon wedding ring.

On 5th July 1989 at about 3.30 pm the bodies of the Dixon's were found on the cliff top at Little Haven. On the very same afternoon Cooper tried to cash in Mr Dixon's wedding ring to Pembroke Jewellers, in Pembroke.

Months later when it had been realized that Mr Dixon's ring had been taken from the murder scene, a detective was sent out to all the places that were likely to buy such a gold ring. A wedding ring
had been cashed in by a member of the public at two places, one in Cardigan and one in Pembroke. The Swansea Court heard evidence about it.

Retired Detective Constable Emlyn Dudley said he knew Cooper in 1989 and had worked on the murder investigation. He said he was told that Mr Dixon's wedding ring was missing and he was ordered to visit all jewellers' shops in the area. He visited 55 in total and found that two members of the public had sold a gold wedding ring shortly after the killings, one in Cardigan and one to Raymond Smith of Pembroke Jewellers, Main Street, Pembroke.

Cooper had sold Mr Dixon's wedding ring to Raymond Smith and had actually signed his name as J Cooper, of 34 St Mary's Park, Jordanston., Cooper's correct address. Mr Dudley said he was told to question Cooper, pretending to investigate the theft of jewellery. At the time, he was aware of the artist's impression. "I probably had it in my pocket all of the time. It did not resemble Cooper," he told the jury. After questioning, Cooper did admit that he had sold a wedding ring at that jewellers on that day. He also admitted that the signature on the paper was his true signature.

When asked by the Police did he take it from Mr Dixon's finger Cooper replied "No, not me". Prosecuting barrister Gerard Elias QC said to Cooper "The ring you sold to Mr Smith was the ring you had taken from Peter Dixon?" Cooper replied: "That's not true."

Asked how it became in his possession and sold by him in Pembroke, Cooper replied that the ring was his own wedding ring. The Police knew this statement was a direct lie. Cooper was still in possession of his own wedding ring up to two years after this date. The Police knew that Cooper still possessed his wedding ring when his daughter got married in 1991.

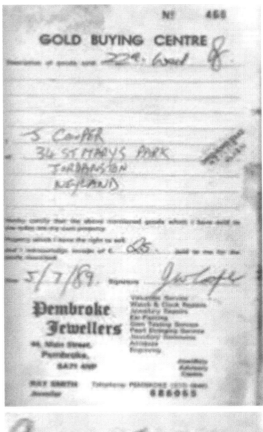

Proof that Cooper sold a Wedding Ring to Ray Smith the
Jeweller in Pembroke, just days after the Dixon Murders.
Cooper told the Police that it was his own wedding ring,
which was a lie. One of his few thing Cooper ever
admitted to was this signature on the ring receipt.
Photograph © Dyfed Powys Police.

On the 5th July at 3.30 pm the bodies of Gwenda and Peter Dixon were discovered . A double murder investigation was commenced later that day. An expert on flies confirmed that they had been dead about six days. Cooper already had a good start on his way to avoid capture. During the investigation the Police interviewed everyone who was in close proximity to the murder site on the day of the killing. They were obviously very interested in anyone walking that part of the cliff path or those that had heard shots that morning. The Pembrokeshire Coastal Footpath is one of the National Trail long distance walks. It stretches along the entire Pembrokeshire Coast National Park, is some 186 miles (299 km) long and is an extremely popular walk. To walk the full length of the path takes up to two weeks Just a half-day outing along the trail is an unforgettable experience. It acts as a reminder that Britain boasts some of the finest coastline in the world. Indeed in 2011 Pembrokeshire was rated as the second best coastal destination in the World, the rating by no less than the National Geographic Society.

Some intrepid visitors decide to run the Pembrokeshire Coast Path, 186 miles, instead of walking it. This could be done in less than a week, and at the time a German holidaymaker was doing just that. On the morning of the murders he was running along the Path, probably within a few miles of Little Haven, but more than likely was nearer to Newgale at the time of the murders. A few hours later he arrived at Whitesands Beach at St David's his feet full of blisters as he was not accustomed to such running. He got talking to the Lifeguards who treated his blisters on his feet. As per protocol for first aid treatments the dutiful Lifeguards logged the home address of the patient, in their daily logbook, before the German went on his way.

When the Police realized they had an address of someone who might have information or who may have heard shots; two detectives were sent to Germany to question the holidaymaker. They questioned the man but he could give them no more information.

The case broke the record for the most phone calls ever provoked by a BBC Crimewatch program, some 1200 incoming calls. Police knocked on every door within a ten mile radius of the murder, traced witnesses all over Britain and Western Europe and took 6,000 statements As a response to a Crimewatch program a lorry driver came forward stating that he had given a lift away from Pembrokeshire toward Neath to a German holidaymaker, a teacher from near Stuttgart who fitted the description of the suspect. After detailed immigration and youth hostel enquiries this second German male was traced. But when detectives questioned him he, too, could tell them nothing.

The Black Bicycle

From Mr Elliott's description of Cooper with his bicycle in Haverfordwest High Street another artist's impression was made but it was 9th July before it was released to the public This E-fit was distributed far and wide and all the investigating team probably carried a copy of it with them. Many of the detectives also knew Cooper but had not connected him at all to the E-fit picture. This is shown when one of the team questioned Cooper about selling a wedding ring, now known to be stolen from Mr Dixon on the day of his murder. This particular part of the investigation was probably carried out many months after the E-fit had been produced and with a clean shaven (except for moustache) face, Cooper, in a relaxed fashion would have looked completely different. This is where the E-fit picture may have thwarted rather than helped the Police investigation. The jury at the Swansea Crown Court trial asked if the bicycle with straight handle bars was ever found. They were provided with an answer in the affirmative saying such a bike was discovered.

A black push bike fitting the description was actually found leaning against the back wall of Flo's, Thornhill house. In Court the jury was told it was found at Cooper's house. If the jury had not asked about the bicycle this fact would not have come to light for the jury or for the public.

The bike noticed by witness Mr Elliot outside the National Westminster Bank in Haverfordwest not only had straight handles like an old bicycle it was also described as black. Although old bicycles (lets say prior to 1967) were invariably black in colour; by 1989 bikes were normally multicoloured. It would have been unusual for a bicycle to be all black. This brings a few factors into play. Either the bicycle was an old one like described or it had been painted black by Cooper. Perhaps both were correct. It could be that this particular bicycle was used by Cooper at night in his nefarious activities and therefore he painted it black, like his shotgun, to make it less conspicuous at night. The author is unaware of what tests were carried out but if the bicycle found looked as if it had been painted then it could have been tested to find out if the black paint on the Dixon shotgun was the same paint as on the bicycle. The Police may have done this as it is known they tested paint in tins found at Cooper's house to relate it to the paint on the Sardis Gun, but it did not match. Some size nine Puma shoes were stolen by Cooper from a house and also painted black. The bicycle, if painted with the same black paint would connect Cooper as the probable person seen extracting money with Mr Dixon's cash card. At the time when Cooper was starting to build a house in Johnston he was banned from driving. For a year he used a bicycle to get around, and confessed to the Police that this same bicycle did have straight handlebars. So we know cycling was not an unusual means of transport for Cooper. The identity of the black old fashioned straight handlebar bicycle was crucial for the Dixon murder investigation. After ten years of putting evidence together, I consider it a bit remiss that the Prosecution were not going to tell the court that they had found it. It is significant that Cooper did not keep this push bike at his own house in St Mary's Park but a mile away at the back of Flo Evans's house at Thornhill, Rosemarket.

The push bike was there when Flo suffered an unusual and suspicious death and was still leaning against the rear wall of her house when the house was being sold by a local Estate Agent, months later. As far as I know it was still there when the house was demolished a few years later. The Swansea jury had to ask in court if the bicycle was ever found and its location was only revealed to the public after this enquiry by an astute juror. When I was considering buying a property in Rosemarket, I looked around Thornhill, the location of Flo's odd death. I have to admit that although I saw a black bicycle there after the Dixon murders it did not trigger any connectivity in my mind with the "Wildman" the Police were looking for. It must be said that in hindsight if a more thorough investigation was done on Flo Evan's bizarre death and the connectivity with Cooper made at that time, the probability is that Cooper would have been incarcerated decades earlier than he was.

The following picture is the Photo e-fit of the "Wildman" who was seen collecting cash with Dixon's Visa card at a Cash Point in both Pembroke and Haverfordwest. The image is particularly accurate. It shows Cooper's distinctive fussy hair and his muscular upper body. What is more surprising is the shorts were recognised by one of the women detectives as looking more like women's shorts than man's shorts. These were the same shorts that Cooper had stolen from Gwenda Dixon's rucksack after her murder on the cliff path just hours before. For a photo fit to get this accuracy from the observations of three witnesses, is, I consider, remarkable.

Photo e-fit of the "Wildman". Given out to the media by the Police ten days after the Dixon bodies had been discovered.

The investigation into looking for a local murderer was severely hampered and diverted by the erroneous notion that a terrorist group, such as the IRA was involved. The killings were certainly an execution type, with obvious torture to extract the bank card pin number and subsequent blasting to death. The location is a remote spot on the Pembrokeshire coast where arms could easily be landed and cached by the IRA. A year long surveillance commenced and a cache was found a few miles further north, but nothing near the Little Haven cliff.

Cooper and the Bullseye TV Game show.

During the late 1980's Cooper was a member of the Darts Team at the Bridgend Inn, Haverfordwest. He also played darts at the Railway Inn in Johnston. You will note these are both near to the railway line that I suspected he used with his bicycles. Cooper was a a regular darts player, inferring that he had reasonable ability for the game. His son Adrian said of his father that he was besotted with the popular "Bullseye" TV Game show. As a potential means of getting some money, and with the added bonus of TV notoriety Cooper managed to get himself on this popular ITV show. Although the public think the show is 'live', it is actually pre-recorded a few weeks or so before. Cooper's appearance on the show was recorded 30th May 1989, exactly one month before the Dixon killings. The show was not televised (screened) until the Sunday before the murders. 22nd June 1989. The ITV film was studied by experts, frame by frame, to see if there was a resemblance of any of the contestants to the artist's impression of the "Wild Man with the bicycle" that had already been issued.

A similarity was found showing Cooper sporting an unusual fuzzy style of hair that had an uncanny likeness to the hair on the artist's impression. The angular shape of the nose is also distinctive. This fuzzy type of hairstyle was in vogue for the fashionable Liverpool football team at the time. To those unaccustomed to seeing this hairstyle it looks more like a wig. Jim Bowen, a comedian and TV presenter hosted the "Bullseye" show from 1981 to 1995. It appealed to a mass audience and was one of the most successful TV game shows ever. There were in excess of 12,000 applications from people wanting to be a contestant each year. The show started in 1981 on a Monday night then changed to a Sunday afternoon and later to Saturday afternoon in 1995.

Cooper was an addict of the show and it would sometimes feature his dart throwing idols of Jocky Wilson, Kieth Dellar and Eric Bristow.

If you study the dates of Cooper's crimes, they would never occur during the "Bullseye" program on television, as he never missed watching the show!

Coopers chance to get on the Game show came in 1989 and he was at the ATV Central Studios at Broad Street, Birmingham on 30th May 1989. The Dixon murders occurred on the Friday after the screening on the Sunday night, one month later. Flo Evans's death was in February of the same year, four months before he was filmed at the ATV studios for the Bullseye Show. This would be the time he was submitting his application to be a contestant on the show.

Darts was Cooper's hobby (not SCUBA diving). He even represented the County of Pembrokeshire once in a trip down to the West Country. I managed to find scorecard of his performance on that occasion; it was similarly disappointing. I think he gets too nervous and is not relaxed enough to play well on the big events. The fact that he played for the County does illustrate that he must have been good at darts at one time. Like many competent players, his darts scored on the TV Game show was abysmal. For such a dart's player, a gambler and being such an addict of the show, it must have been the ultimate disappointed for Cooper to walk away with nothing. He was actually given a lifeline in the show and he even lost the second time as well. This is where the press nicknames for Cooper has come from; "The Game Show Killer" and the "Bullseye Killer" The author is convinced that his inability to perform well on the show, prompted the Dixon murders. Cooper must have been completely down hearted and depressed to be humiliated publicly on the Game Show. He needed a boost. Cooper had to show the world and prove to himself that he was an expert at something. His **unusual hobby**, was what he was good at, we are not talking about SCUBA but killing people and getting away with it. By losing on the Bullseye Game Show, the scene had been set for another double killing. This killing was at Little Haven, in a predetermined hiding place, just five days after the Bullseye Show was televised. Prior to the recording session for the ITV Game-show each contestant must write their own profile giving their address and what hobbies and interests they have. This gives a bit of depth and helpful prompts which the host, Jim Bowen, can refer to when they appear before the cameras.

Cooper probably wrote these details on his application form some months prior to May 1989. These details would have helped the TV company pick the four Pembrokeshire contestants. On the show the host, Jim Bowen, picks up the appropriate prompt card and asks 'John from Milford Haven', " you have an unusual hobby, John, don't You?" Cooper replies "Oh. Yes !", Cooper is smiling and enjoying his devious and strange answer but then carries on to say that his hobby is 'SCUBA diving.' Cooper's second answer, even if true, was not regarded at the time *an unusual hobby.* There were more than 130 people living in Pembrokeshire who had the same hobby. The term SCUBA, (Self Contained Breathing Apparatus) was old fashioned and an Americanism. It was a word rarely used by those enjoying amateur diving in the UK in 1989. Participants would more commonly refer to the sport as Sub Aqua or Sports Diving. Any recreational diver or amateur diver, who thought they had an unusual hobby would have been more specific, ie they would say "they photographed sea slugs" or "enjoyed wreck diving " or "hunted mermaids". Being more specific these hobbies could be termed *unusual.* Certainly not the sport itself.

Analysing Cooper's reply the more odd it becomes. It endorses two facts, that he actually did little Sub Aqua diving, but more significantly he was secretly thinking about his other more sinister hobby. He had managed to get onto the Game Show by saying he had an unusual hobby, but was not stupid enough to tell the world at large what his unusual hobby actually was! (I am a serial killer!) As with his Police interview Cooper is adept at giving devious and plausible answers. He is boastful and thinks it will appeal to the audience but it certainly was not his correct hobby. The reply was more full of deceit than of accuracy or truth.

The Conviction

Cooper was convicted of the murder mainly on the grounds that a glove he was wearing at the time left fibres on the twigs that he had broken and cut to hide the bodies. The same glove fibres were discovered on a shotgun also belonging to Cooper. Traces of Dixon's blood were found beneath black paint on a shotgun discovered at Cooper's house.

Another damming piece of evidence was the realization that
Cooper had kept a pair of shorts from the Dixon murder scene.
A pair of green shorts, had been retained by Cooper as a trophy. The
hemline had been altered so that they fitted him and the shorts were
found in the bedroom at 34 St Mary's Park. Jordanston. On the
shorts were found tiny traces of Peter Dixon's blood. Also under the
altered hem were found DNA material that belonged to their daughter,
Julie. It was a major mistake for Cooper to retain souvenirs, and
garments of his murdered victims. The evidence they contained were
to prove his guilt. Cooper wore gloves to avoid fingerprints but he
was not to know that forensic science of clothing and glove fibres
years later would be equally as incriminating as fingerprints.
In the summing up at Swansea Crown Court the judge said:
"Mr and Mrs Dixon had to wait for immediate execution and
the one was forced to watch as the other was murdered in cold blood
knowing the other would soon face the same thing."
During the ongoing investigation, one of the largest ever conducted by
any Police Force, Kevin Dixon, said of his grief about his brother's
murder; "You don't come to terms with grief, you carry it discreetly
but it leaves a mark. "We would like to see somebody brought to
account. It doesn't make our loss any better or easier to carry but it
will give us a sense of closure."
A profile of this incident, compared to other Cooper crimes .
Two adults killed.
A brutal attack, blood everywhere.
Sawn-off shotgun used at close quarters.
Cord used to tie hands.
Someone immensely strong involved
Both bodies moved after death
Bodies hidden in undergrowth as per SAS Handbook.
Bodies concealed to delay discovery.
No incriminating fingerprints
No obvious motive, lower clothing removed.
A rural and preplanned location
No shotgun found, no cartridges found
Glove fibres found on twigs.
Within 6 miles of where Cooper was living.

Tooze Murders - Unresolved Murder Enquiry
Date: 26th July 1993
Location: Ty ar y Waun Farmhouse. Llanharry, Bridgend,
Glamorgan
Who died. Meg Tooze, Harry Tooze and another male. Possibly
the missing man James Stead.
Outcome: Unresolved, but being treated as a Double Murder,
not a triple murder. Harry Tooze has never been found.

At Llanharry in Vale of Glamorgan in July 1993 there were two people found shot at close range with a shotgun. Their bodies were hidden under bales of hay and a carpet in a old cowshed. It is one of Wales's long standing murder mysteries and bears all the hallmarks of Cooper. All the other murders and suspicious deaths mentioned in this book occurred in Pembrokeshire, within the Dyfed Powys Police Force. These murders occurred near Bridgend, a few miles from the Headquarters of the South Wales Police Force. It is more than obvious from the evidence available in the public domain that the South Wales Police Force not only botched the investigation, put an innocent man in jail for the crime, but were complicit in hiding the truth from the Coroner, the Ross Report, the family involved and the public. The South Wales Police and the detectives involved, some of whom have committed and admitted perjury, know the main facts of the case but are not likely to come forward with the truth as there is far more for them to lose than to gain by doing so. A Ross Report, an independent report in lieu of a Public Enquiry, into the handling of the Tooze Investigation, has been kept secret from the public, despite Freedom of Information requests. It should not be the prerogative of the same South Wales Police to block this Report from being seen.
 In 2001, the Assistant Chief of Police admitted this report showed that the investigating officers were not up to scratch and that it had revealed new evidence. That new evidence has never been revealed despite tax payers money being spent to retrieve it. The report is so damaging to the Police Force and its now retired officers that it is being blocked from public view.

History has now determined that the South Wales Police Force was the most corrupt Police Force in the UK from 1988 to 2000.
During that time they convicted no less than 8 innocent men for murders they did not commit. Members of Parliament demanded that this Police Force should have been disbanded and it is a great injustice that five senior officers were not themselves put behind bars in 2011 when Britain's biggest police corruption trial collapsed. Some of these same officers were deeply involved with the Tooze Murder investigations when it is themselves that should have been under investigation. The Police Corruption Trial cost the public £30 million pounds. The ongoing investigation into the Llanharry Murders, now in its 24th year, an estimated further £20 million pounds.
The Tooze murders in July 1993 at Llanharry, Glamorgan, do bear a striking resemblance to Cooper's four established murders. Especially as a double murder with a double barrelled shotgun at close quarters. This type of murder is unusual in Wales. It is extremely unfortunate that so much of the evidence has been corrupted, with false statements from both Police and witnesses. The Police and neighbours may genuinely not know who the murderer was, but their false evidence, together with the fact that Harry Tooze's body was taken away from the murder scene, has not helped in establishing the truth.

A profile and comparisons to Cooper's murders.
Two adults killed, possibly three. Brutal killings.
Double barrelled shotgun used at point blank range.
No murder weapon found and no spent cartridges found.
Two bodies moved after death and hidden.
Bodies concealed to delay discovery.
House fully locked up and pet inside.
Shotgun stolen from house months before
Semi remote location surrounded by fields.
No unusual fingerprints found. No obvious motive .
Neighbours who found bodies not properly investigated.
Like Mr Richards at Scoverston, Harry Tooze sold bales of hay.
Dubious Coroner's decision.

Mount Estate Attack.
Date: 6th March 1996
Location: in fields near Mount Estate, Milford Haven.
Who involved : Five teenagers, three girls and two boys.
Crime: Rape, sexual assault, Attempted Armed Robbery.
Outcome: Cooper found guilty in 2011.

It was early evening and the light had faded fast as five teenagers were walking near a wood in Milford Haven. They were between 15 and 16 years of age, minding their own business, when they were suddenly confronted by a masked man brandishing a shotgun and a torch. He had on a long wax coat and was accompanied with a dog. The attack was in a wooded area near fields at the back of the Mount Estate in Milford Haven. The attacker confronted them from the front shining the torch in their faces and at gunpoint took them to a low lying part of the field, that was out of earshot of children playing at the Mount Estate. The attacker ordered them all to lie down on the ground, face down and give him their ages and names. There were two boys and three girls. The man, we now know to be John Cooper, was extremely violent, kicking and hitting the group and even butting one in the head with the gun. The group was, understandably so extremely frightened that they obeyed and would not move. At gunpoint he demanded money from each of them, but they said they had none. When one of the boys moved he was kicked and told to get his head back down. They were also told that if they did not move, none of them would be hurt. By the hair, Cooper took one of the girls aged 16 to land nearby. At knife point he told her to remove one leg from her jeans. There are two interesting new facts that come to light about Cooper from this attack. One is that there is mention of a dog with Cooper. If it is Cooper's own dog then identifying the dog may have been an easier option for the investigating Police than to trace the attacker. However, if Cooper thought the Police could trace him via his dog, it is quite possible that Cooper would kill the dog the following day to make his identity less obvious. A year after I wrote the last sentence I am told that Cooper dug a small trench in his garden and got his own dog to sit next to it while he shot it dead. Perhaps this happened the day after the Mount Estate Attack.

The others could hear the girl crying and pleading "Please don't !". Cooper told her to stop crying, shut up and not to tell anyone otherwise he would kill her. Then he raped her with a knife on the ground next to her head., and the shotgun lying next to them on the ground. After about ten minutes he told the girl to get dressed and not to tell anyone. Both of them then returned to the group, when the same boy was kicked again. Cooper then got one of the other girls to stand while he, kneeling, put his hand up her front to feel her breasts and then down her track suit bottoms to touch her intimately. The others during this time stayed on the ground trembling in fear. He demanded money again, but was only offered a watch and an empty wallet from one of the boys. He then ordered them all to walk slowly away from the site and not look back at him. Cooper shouted that they were not to tell anyone otherwise he would kill them. The words reported as "I know who you are and will come to kill you if you tell anyone." As he left through the hedges, he fired a shot off from the shotgun into the air as if to reinforce his threat. As soon as members of the group got back to their homes, their parents and the Police were informed. Some time later Police searched the area for the spent cartridge from this shot, but failed to find any cartridge. Like the situation at Scoveston and the Dixon murders no cartridges were ever found. Police were later aware that Cooper had burgled at least two houses in the vicinity over the previous few weeks and it was quite possible he was looking at other houses to burgle when, by accident he bumped into the five teenagers. Two of the local houses of the 30 burglaries that Mr Cooper was convicted of occurred on the 10th and 23rd February 1996 close to these Mount Estate fields. The attack could not have been planned and Cooper's actions must have been instantaneous, unlike other crimes of his that show considerable preplanning. The order of events in this attack are significant. As with his other crimes it commences with Cooper completely paralysing with fear his victims by using his voice and frightening posture with his gun. He is then demanding money and once he has complete control of his assailants it excites him sexually so he continues to dominate by completing a sexual act.

The other fact to emerge is that Cooper was carrying a large knife with him, and together with the shotgun used it to threaten with. We do not see the use of a knife as a threatening weapon in his other crimes; although it may have been part of the assault for which he attended Borstal Reform School as a youth. We know a knife was used to cut small branches and bracken to conceal the Dixon bodies. Cooper is following the SAS Survival Handbook advice that a knife is the first thing that a commando should always have with him. Two bush knives were stolen by Cooper from an unoccupied bungalow not far from the Mount Estate in October 1995. A security light being kept on in the house was no deterrent for Cooper whatsoever. The sheath of one of these knives was recovered in 1996 on the fields between the Sardis armed burglary and Cooper's house. The gun that Cooper had used in the Mount Estate attack was described in detail by the teenage boys as a side by side shotgun with a lanyard attached. It is possible that this was the first night that Cooper had this particular gun with him. The gun is thought to be the one which had been stolen by Cooper in a house burglary at Castle Pill on 1st March 1996, this is only five days before this incident. If the same gun then in those five days Cooper has already sawn the barrels to shorten the gun and also added the lanyard and clips to it. This gun, nicknamed the Duck Run Gun by the Police was found under the mud in the back garden of Cooper's house. Cooper's Defence brought up a significant anomaly in the witness statements about the physique of the man in the Mount Estate incident. The teenagers said that the man was skinny and the one who was raped said her attacker was only about 7 stone in weight. Cooper at the time was twice this weight and would be described as heavily built. How could the witnesses be so wrong in their description? It is recognized that witness reports may have inaccuracies and that they only have only 50% reliability. It was dark, the victim was frightened for her life and the attacker was wearing a long wax coat. The girl that was raped could only guess her attackers weight by knowing the weight of a 44 kilo (7 stone) person on top of her. Cooper may have rested half his weight on his elbows during the rape, giving the girl the impression that her

All the witnesses saw Cooper from a low ground level. This coupled with the frightening effect of a dark balaclava and the fact that he wore a long trench coat may have given them the idea that he was skinny and tall. The fact that the attacker had a shotgun, wore a balaclava and gloves are certainly the hallmark of Cooper. Also the gun was used to hit one of the male teenagers on the head, a signature of Cooper's brutality and aggression also seen with Gwenda Dixon and with Sheila Clarke in the Sardis Armed Burglary.

Detectives involved with the case consider that these teenagers were fortunate that they were so passive during the attack. The Police are of the opinion that if they had retaliated Cooper would have not hesitated in using his shotgun to kill all five of them. Cooper's Defence said that there was no evidence of rape and that this charge should be reduced to one of sexual assault. The Prosecution, however, could prove that fibres found on a glove belonging to Cooper were found inside the clothing of one of the attacked girls.

At Cardiff Crown Court in 2011, details of the rape, assault and attempted burglary were given. One of the girls involved gave evidence, to hide her identity she gave her evidence behind a screen at the Court. In January 2011 one of the three girls involved in the attack tragically died before she could attend the Crown Court and give her evidence. The judge did however allow a previously recorded video of her evidence to be given in Court although it was impossible for her to be cross-examined by Cooper's Defence. The attack had seriously affected her mentally and had caused depression in her life. She was stressed at having to go through the ordeal in Court and died of an overdose of her prescribed drugs before it happened. Whether such was an accidental overdose or deliberate, we can only guess, but her morphine blood concentration was ten times higher than that which would give cardio respiratory failure.

It is so sad that she was not alive four months later to hear of the Cooper conviction. Her life and those of her affected family add more victims of misery caused by Cooper's crimes. Crimes that he will never admit to and crimes to which he is unrepentant. The attack, because no money was extracted was technically an attempted armed robbery on five people, together with one rape and a sexual assault. The two boys who were part of the attack at the Mount Estate, were also traumatized, to such an extent that they did not like going out at night, even 15 years later.

The most damming evidence against Cooper for this crime was the fact that the Forensic laboratory found two fibres in the knickers of one of the girl's. It was glove fibre belonging to a glove that had belonged to Cooper. It was fortunate that tapings from the clothing of the rape victim and the girl sexually assaulted had been taken by Forensic officers. Also that these had been sealed and kept for over 15 years.

Gerard Elias QC, Prosecuting at Swansea Crown Court mentioned that the fibre transfer from the single glove was the only thing found to connect this rape with the other Cooper murders. However the connection to Cooper was compelling. The attacker wore a long wax jacket, army style boots, dark gloves and a balaclava. He also had a bush knife and a sawn off shotgun and uttered similar words similar to Cooper in the Sardis armed robbery. Apart from the jacket and boots, the same clothing as the attacker seen in the Sardis attack for which Cooper had already been found guilty. Three out of the five teenagers identified Cooper's voice correctly in a Voice Recognition Identification Test.

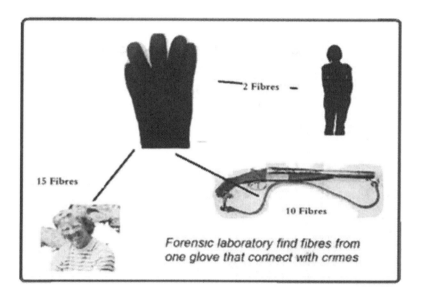

15 Fibres

2 Fibres

10 Fibres

Forensic laboratory find fibres from one glove that connect with crimes

Factors involved in a profile of this incident, compared to other known crimes associated with Cooper.

Hooded man terrifies using voice and shotgun

Five teenagers ambushed and controlled.

A ferocious attack, getting dark, early evening.

Money demanded and threatened with knife and shotgun

The shotgun had a lanyard as found at Cooper's house.

Attacker wearing dark gloves and dark balaclava

Glove fibres prove sexual assault .

Gun butt struck on the head of one of the victims.

Shotgun fired but no cartridge found.

A rural isolated field .

Motive: robbery, domination, sexual gratification.

Sardis Shotgun Robbery
Date: 22nd November 1996
Location: Sardis, Near Rosemarket, Pembrokeshire
Outcome: Cooper convicted for this crime in December 1998.

It was a Friday evening in November 1996 when schoolteacher Sheila Clarke (Wilkins book spells her name Clark) was relaxing in her bungalow in Sardis. It was early evening and she was by herself in the house watching television. On the television was an appeal for 'Children in Need Day'. Her husband was due to return to the house at any time and she started pouring a glass of wine to greet him with. She then heard a noise near the front door but realized it was not her husband as she had not heard any car turn up outside. She explained to Police, "It had been Children in Need Day and my first thought was it could have been a Sixth Former come to demand money, I soon realized it was not." You can imagine her shock and horror when, through the living room door burst a masked man wielding a shotgun.

It was Cooper who in a violent and aggressive preplanned move is shouting " I want money". Mrs Clarke is led to the bedroom where Cooper commences to tie her up with a piece of rope he has brought with him. Cooper may have demanded to know where she hides her money and jewellery. With years of experience in robbing houses, he may not need to ask, he knows all the places where people hide their money and jewellery. Cooper finds and steals jewellery to the value of about £6,000. During the attack Cooper twice hits Mrs Clarke in the face and also uses his gun to hit her on the head. He also throws a small portable 12 volt television at her. As he is about to leave or decide what to do with Mrs Clarke, she manages to wriggle one arm free from her bondage and press the panic button of her alarm system.

The alarm may automatically give out a loud siren noise, or Cooper may have seen her press the button. Mrs Clarke may have told Cooper that the alarm had been pressed and that the Police would be arriving at any moment. Cooper panicked. He was no longer in control and quickly ran out of the house, across fields back to his home, only 800 meters away.

Mrs Clarke had a Piper Lifeline System, an alarm system which could be hired from the County Council. As a teacher she was on the County Council payroll. This system provides a mobile panic button pendant that can be worn around the neck or hung near a bed that automatically sends a wireless signal through the land line telephone. The number automatically connects with the Ambulance or Emergency Control Centre or the 999 system. Even if two way speech is not possible the Control Centre operator can immediately see on a computer screen the house address that has activated it. The system also has a neighbour or local contact number for the Emergency Services to notify. This system was certainly was a lifeline and probably saved Mrs Clarke from being another of Cooper's murder victims.

Fortunately a neighbour saw a man wearing a balaclava running away from the house. Later a Police tracker dog followed the route the attacker had taken. It took them straight to Cooper's house.

It was on this trail that various incriminating items were found, discarded in a hurry by Cooper who did not want to be caught possessing them. These items were used as critical evidence in Cooper's Swansea Court case. The following day the Police were doing house to house questioning. Cooper, being a resident in the neighbourhood was amongst those interviewed. As cool as anything Cooper said his dog was barking at the time and it must have been the robber running past his house! The items discarded by Cooper included a balaclava, a sawn off shotgun (then nick- named the Sardis Trail Gun), a pair of Puma shoes, and one glove.

Although this incident in 1996 traumatized Sheila Clarke, she nevertheless agreed to and attended the Cardiff Court Trial in 2011. In tears she related the incident again to a new jury who needed convincing that Cooper was indeed a murderer. Despite being extremely stressful for her she realized that relating her experience once again was going to be important for the Prosecution, and so it proved to be.

Factors involved in a profile of this incident.
One adult female alone in a house.
Evening attack.
Cooper intrudes into the house and frightens the occupant
Money demanded
Victim tied to her bed with pre-knotted cord.
Victims head is covered with clothing
Cooper hits her three times, once with his shot gun. Cooper
known to have sawn off shotgun and a bush knife. Shotgun
has a lanyard attached
Cooper wears dark coloured gloves and a balaclava
Jewellery worth £6,000 pounds stolen.
Cooper flees when alarm activated.
Panic and run, shown by Cooper.
Cooper discards incriminating clothing and tools.
House has fields at the back.
House only 800 meters from Cooper's home.
Shotgun, glove, balaclava and jemmy recovered.

Two years later Cooper was convicted of this armed robbery.
He was sentenced for 16 years for this robbery and another 30
other burglaries carried out in the Milford Haven area.
He served ten years and was in prison from 1998 to 2008. The
crime figures around the Milford Haven area where Cooper
used to live diminished to an all time low.   It was a relief for
the Milford Haven Police as their crime figures suddenly
dropped. However other officers were starting to investigate if
this same man was responsible for the two double murders that
were still unsolved.

Needless to say, all murders, rapes and robberies happening in
Wales during the time Cooper was behind bars cannot be
attributed to him!

Death of Pat Cooper, regarded as a natural death.
Date: December 2008
Location : In her bungalow in Letterston, Pembrokeshire.
Cooper is released from prison on 28th September 2008 and after
spending over two months in a hostel is reunited with his wife. While
at the Swansea hostel, Cooper does everything asked of him. This
includes no alcohol, a night curfew and reporting his presence every
two hours. He knows he is being watched carefully by the Police and
that he has to conform; it is a rehabilitation period before being
allowed back to Pembrokeshire. During this time he was forbidden to
see his wife or his son. The Police, suspecting Cooper of already being
a serial killer have spent six months preparing for the date when
Cooper is to be released on parole. When he returns to his wife, the
Police may even have bugged his house to listen to their first
conversations. The house is a Council semi-detached bungalow in
Letterston, about 5 miles south of Fishguard. A policeman is
positioned along the street watching the house where Cooper and his
wife are spending their first night. Cooper has been confined in prison
and this is the first time he is spending private time with his wife in
over ten years. At 3.15 am in the morning Cooper rings 999 the
emergency services saying that his wife, Pat, has died. The Police are
informed but allow the Ambulance crew to take away her body to the
hospital. It is more than obvious to one and all that this again is
Cooper silencing someone who holds vital evidence to convict him of
murder. The Police arrange for Cooper to stay with his brother
allowing them access to the Letterston house to do some investigation.
Steve Wilkins, the one in charge of investigating Cooper mentions in
his book that he told the Pathologist to look carefully at the body to
see if there were signs of violence or a suspicious death.

That is what the Pathologist is trained to do and needs no advice from a detective who has already allowed Pat's body and all the vital evidence of a suspicious death or potential murder scene to be disturbed.

When the Ambulance crew were removing Pat's body from the house, Cooper made a point of telling the Paramedics that he and his wife had had a bath together then they went to bed and made love. His wife was grasping for breath in the middle of the night and then she died. He then telephoned 999. The Home Office Pathologist found no bruising or marks of strangulation or suffocation, but he did find a distressed and engorged heart, suggesting a heart attack or heart disease condition. Pat's family had a history of heart problems and her death was thought to be a combination of that and her just giving up, unable to start life again with her husband. This was the opinion of both Steve Wilkins and members of Cooper's family, conveniently dismissing the extremely suspicious circumstances. Once again the Police are giving Cooper the benefit of the doubt and treat the whole incident with compassion. As the verdict of the Pathologist was that there were no signs of violence the Police continued to treat it as a natural occurrence and with respect to the family did not pursue any murder enquiry. One has to be suspicious and consider if Cooper had planned the death of his wife for months. He had received four days of questioning by the Police when in custody in July 2008, only six months before returning to his wife. The questioning was specifically about the Dixon and Scoveston murders, he knew that his wife was going to be asked similar questions by the Police. He also knew that she could give different answers and incriminate him without her realizing it. For instance if the Police asked her had she ever been to Howelston Camping site, where the Dixons had been camping, it would be hard for her to say no, when in fact she regularly cleaned the caravans there. She had also supplied curtains and cushions to caravan owners at the site. Cooper had years in prison to think of ways to murder someone without detection. He was already an expert at this before being put in prison. On the Bullseye Show Cooper made a boast about being a diver. Air embolism is a subject studied in sub aqua training, and would be understood by Cooper.

Both Caisson's Disease (The Bends) and Air Embolism produce clots to form in the blood causing death in severe cases. Such would cause a distressed and engorged heart as found by the Pathologist investigating Pat Cooper's condition."When the embolism enters a vein, it is called a venous air embolism, when air enters an artery, it is called an arterial air embolism. These air bubbles can travel to your brain, heart, or lungs and cause a heart attack, stroke or respiratory failure." (www. Healthline.com).

A year before Cooper left prison there was an article on the Internet explaining about death due to air embolism, and although rare, that it could be caused during sex. If Cooper was looking for such an article on the Internet, he surely would have seen it when he was behind bars. He may have planned his wife's death from this time. This then ties in with him making sure he mentions he has had sex with his wife before her death. We know that Cooper was keen to understand medical conditions as one of the items he stole from a house on 22nd December 1995   was a a Nursing Times book,. It was discovered at Cooper's house when they tore it apart while he was in prison.

His diver knowledge made him aware that a needle injection of air would cause an air embolism. However this would not cause certain death and would probably be detected by a Pathologist. A more certain way of death would be to inject talcum powder or smoke. The white blood corpuscles attack the foreign bodies of the dust particles and air that is injected and those themselves add to a clot to form in the blood. Death would occur when blood does not circulate, the heart goes into overdrive and the victim gasps for breath before death. Grasping for breath is how Cooper himself describes how Pat died. The Pathologist would have carefully looked at the possibility of asphyxia. A murder caused by smothering using a pillow or cushion to suffocate. Although signs of violence may not be seen the Pathologist must have ruled this out. However the Pathologist is unlikely to notice a pin prick on a corpse, especially if he is not specifically looking for one.

Cooper would probably have realized that to induce an air embolism was the only way to kill his wife without detection.

He had to act fast before his wife was called for questioning. Like his other victims, she needed to be silenced. Forensic Pathologists are trained to look for signs of copulation on bodies. In the case of Pat Cooper there was no evidence that Cooper had had sex with his wife on the night of her death. This in itself makes Cooper's deception more plausible. I consider that Cooper once again got away with murder. If so, this time it was under the very noses of a whole Police team who suspected him of being a serial killer. Pat Cooper was well liked in the community. She kept and bred horses for members of the Pembrokeshire Hunt, which included many of the gentry farmers, local judges and top society of Pembrokeshire. Pat had given evidence at the Huntsman Trial, which actually contradicted a previous statement of hers. When Cooper was in prison, the Police suspected him of the Scoveston and Dixon murders. That was the time the Police should have formally questioned Pat about her husband's activities in relationship with those murders. Because the Police did not want to implicate Pat with Cooper's crimes, this was never done. The consequence of this was that it protracted the collection of evidence against Cooper for another decade and probably cost Pat her life.

Factors involved in a profile of this incident, compared to other Cooper crimes .
One adult, Cooper's wife died in bed in the middle of the night.
In Cooper's home, a semi-detached bungalow in Letterston.
No signs of violence found on Pat's body and nothing incriminating found.
Pathologist found a heart engorged and over activated. Pathologist stated Pat's heart showed three conditions that could have caused her death.
Motive would be to silence his wife before she gave incriminating evidence to the Police.
Cooper deliberately lies to the Paramedics as to what happened to thwart and confuse any further investigation.

Cooper's admissions and denials.

Over a span of thirty years of Police questioning and replies under oath in Court there have been a few admissions, but very few. When hundreds of burgled items were displayed he said they were not stolen by him, "except four". Cooper says he was not the masked man in the Sardis robbery yet the balaclava and jacket seen by the witness was found in a hedge near Cooper's house. Jacket fibres found in Cooper's shed and hair belonging to Cooper was found inside the balaclava. Cooper then admits the balaclava was his but it had been stolen from his boat. Gloves found by the police at his house, Cooper said, belonged to his son. When the Police found jewellery or stolen goods in his house taken from his burglaries, Cooper would reply that his wife had bought the goods or they belonged to his wife or daughter.

A Prison Probation officer once asked Cooper why he committed the burglary crimes. He confessed that he had a gambling habit. Since that time he venomously denies saying this to anybody and says he never had a gambling problem. Perhaps, Cooper regarded gambling as a habit, but to him it was not a problem !

Cooper has admitted that for four years from 1992 he did deal in stolen goods, but says they were not stolen by him. He admits he knew a "fair bit about shotguns".

After many denials of ever having been to Scoveston Manor, Cooper eventually admitted that he had visited Scoveston Manor, "a couple of times". In reality he worked for Richard Thomas and Richard Thomas's brother. He denied ever going near Little Haven and later confessed that he went fishing from there and had sold mackerel in the village.

During his questioning, he was always diverting blame on to his son. Cooper always wished to discredit his son or to lay blame in that direction. During his prison term, Cooper even came up with a story that another person from Pembroke Dock had done the 'Milford Murders' meaning Scoveston. When the Police checked the story they found that the man involved could not have done the Scoveston Murders as the man was in prison on that date.

113

Throughout his Swansea Court Case he continuously denied knowing anything about the Scoveston Murders, the Dixon Murders and the Mount Estate attacks saying he was not responsible. He also defiantly said he had wrongly been convicted in 1998 for the 30 burglaries and the Sardis Armed Robbery. He said he was angry at being wrongly imprisoned for ten years. Apart from denying things when initially asked he also had clever answers when pushed. He was asked about his shoe size and he answered size 8. In fact shoes and Wellington boots at Cooper's house were all size 9. The Police knew his shoe size was 9 as footwear had been stolen during his burglaries on three occasions, all Size 9. A pair of Puma trainers was stolen from a house and Cooper was known to have painted them black before using them. The Court established to the jury that Cooper was a compulsive liar, they could also have proved that he continuously deceived the Police.

The forensic evidence that proved guilt.
During the two decades since the murders considerable innovations and improvements had developed in forensic science. Tests were carried out from 1998 to 2009 on items mainly found at Cooper's home in St Mary's Place, Jordanston, a week after he was put in custody. The fibres from Cooper's gloves were to provide strong links with all the murders and the rape. Although strong links but because only a few minute hair like fibres were involved, many have been critical that the evidence itself is far too minute to be of paramount importance to prove guilt. However it is universally accepted that Cooper is justifiably convicted on all counts and deserves the sentence of life imprisonment.
A blood sample on shorts found at Cooper's house were attributed to the Dixon family and a sock belonging to Richard Thomas found near Cooper's house had Cooper's glove fibres in it.
On the Sardis shotgun (the one that the Police should have destroyed after his first trial) the barrels had been painted over with black paint. The forensic laboratory actually found incriminating evidence beneath this paint. Beneath the black paint tiny flakes of blood were discovered which matched Peter Dixon's DNA.

Of interest, we are told that Cooper whilst he was in prison would often study details and cases involving DNA. He was probably researching the subject so that he could combat any critical questioning from the Police.

The gun that showed this DNA evidence should have been destroyed by the Police after Cooper's first Trial. They had been ordered to do so by Judge Moreton. The fact that it was not destroyed was both an embarrassment and a blessing. The Police were keen for this fact not to be mentioned and nothing about it was heard in the Swansea Trial. Cooper's outburst to the Court at the end of his trial may relate to this. He was aggrieved about something saying that elements of his defence had not been heard by the jury. Altogether the forensic evidence was so huge that the jury gave a unanimous decision of guilty on all counts. After the verdict, trial judge Mr Justice Griffith Williams told Cooper: "These murders were all such evil wickedness that the mandatory sentence of life imprisonment will mean just that". Unrepentant Cooper shouted to the Court from the dock, "This is rubbish, utter rubbish! The jury has been on the Internet. I don't blame them but evidence has been held from them ".

An eight week trial at Swansea Crown Court found John William Cooper guilty of two double murders, a rape, a sexual attack and five attempted armed robberies. On 26 May 2011 he was sentenced to four life sentences . Additionally Mr Justice Williams said it was academic but Cooper would serve 15 years for the rape, eight years for the indecent assault and seven years for the attempted robberies (The Mount Estate attack). Cooper was aged 66 in 2011 and is never likely to be released from jail. Cooper has continued to deny all charges ever made against him. He has been defiant and mentioned his anger at having been imprisoned for ten years for crimes he says he knew nothing about.

To demonstrate how dangerous a man Cooper was, Dr Adrian West s forensic psychologist, made the comment to the Police that there were only two people he would not like to see in his bedroom at night, knowing he would have to kill them to survive, one was Donald Neilson and the other John Cooper.

The Judge, Mr Justice Griffith Williams told Cooper, "I'm confident you will never express any remorse to help those who have lost loved ones to come to terms with what has happened. "You are a very dangerous man, a highly organized and predatory burglar whose hallmarks were using a balaclava, gloves and a sworn-off shotgun that was loaded and that you were ready to use, if necessary."
"If it had not been for advances in forensic science you may never have been brought to justice because your offences were well planned, allowing you to evade arrest for so long."

The emotional and financial cost to the community.
Chief Superintendent Dean Richards, Commander for the Pembrokeshire Division, Dyfed Powys Police, said: "The crimes John William Cooper has been convicted of are among the most serious and the worst ever perpetrated in Pembrokeshire. These terrible events have shocked and appalled people across the county. Serious crimes especially murders are extremely rare in Pembrokeshire and people have understandably been frightened and concerned. Mr Cooper's conviction I hope will enable the victims their families, and all those affected by these awful crimes, to finally draw a line under these tragic events in the full knowledge that the man responsible will spend the rest of his life behind bars." Detective Chief Superintendent Steve Wilkins, who had been involved for more than five years, reminded the public that Cooper on his arrest in 2009 had shouted out " Don't judge me until after the evidence has been heard" he said that the evidence has now been heard and this evil man has been found guilty, the correct decision, in his opinion." He thanked the victims and families of the victims for their cooperation in the investigation and the trial.
The total cost of the Cooper investigation is difficult to assess but must run into many millions of pounds. The Forensics alone cost £1.5 million pounds. The consequence of Cooper being kept in prison for the rest of his days another £45,000 per year.

For the Dixon murder investigation alone it took 8,001 days to finally convict the culprit. During this time 30,707 documents, some over 100 pages, were produced. Altogether an estimated 1.5 to 2 million pieces of paper. This gives widely differing number of fir trees pulped for the paper but roughly 15 to 50 trees used to make the paper for these documents. Added to this is all the documents and questionnaires for the Scoveston and Mount Estate attack which may have another 750,000 pieces of paper.

Is Cooper innocent?

John Cooper has always said he is innocent of all the charges made against him, not only the two double murders, the sexual attacks, but all his armed robberies and burglaries. When he was serving his original sentence Cooper said that he would not admit anything in prison to help him get parole as he had not committed the crimes in the first place. With insurmountable evidence against him there is little doubt that Cooper has continually lied to evade capture and to avoid being proved guilty. There remains one member of his family, Wayne Cooper, a nephew, that is far from convinced of Cooper's guilt on all his crimes. The Forensic Science Service has now been disbanded through lack of Government funding but there was some concern amongst members of the public that Cooper's guilt rested on such minute fibres. One person commented on a forum after the sentencing saying " What appals me is the use of microscopic amounts of evidence. Scratch your head, get stopped by a policeman, who then goes to attend a crime scene contaminated with your DNA. He (Cooper) probable did the crime, however to rely on on such flimsy evidence is absurd."

One has to have an empathy with the writer of this comment. The green shorts were a key evidence item and the Prosecution at first suggested that they belonged to Julie Dixon (not Gwenda Dixon) because DNA found on the shorts matched hers. When questioned about ownership Julie said she did not recognize them.

It was later explained that any clothing handled in the Dixon household could show DNA of other members of the family.
The fibres that convicted Cooper were so minute they could hardly be seen with the naked eye. As the defence pointed out, the same black gloves would have been manufactured in their thousands. How is one to believe the credibility of scientists who say they identified blood belonging to a certain individual after it has had black paint chemicals embedded on top of it for 15 or more years? It must be true, but I for one, find it hard to believe. The scientists stated that it was the paint itself that had helped preserve the evidence.

Those affected by Cooper

We must never forget the immense effect that Cooper's crimes have caused to others. Not only to the immediate families of the victims, to Cooper's own family but on the whole community of Pembrokeshire.
Chief Superintendent Wilkins mentioned that it had a negative effect on the tourist trade of the area and had even caused some to move house. The crimes were a constant talking point and concern for the people of Pembrokeshire for decades. When I started writing this within a few months of the Cooper conviction, friends closest to me refused to talk to me about what they knew of Cooper, their memories still too painful. When I looked at the names of people mentioned in the text, The Fire Officers, who attended at Scoverston, the earlier Detectives and names of those affected, I was astonished to realize how many of them I have known throughout my years of living in Pembrokeshire. One realizes, like with modern day Facebook followers, that whole communities are intricately woven. In some way, I expect Cooper's actions have placed a burden on each one of us, either financially or emotionally or both. Many millions of pounds have been spent by the taxpayers of Dyfed over Police salaries, the cost of court cases and investigations into Cooper over the years. Hundreds of homeowners have had their houses burgled and their most treasured possessions stolen. The emotional cost is as enormous as the financial costs.

The attacks by Cooper left immense psychological scars on the Milford Haven teenagers and Sheila Clarke. Horrific memories that haunt their lives forever. If there is no remorse from Cooper himself, there must be huge guilt remaining for his son and daughter. Leaving the Crown Court early were family members of Cooper who still believed in his innocence. To the other family members of Richard and Helen Thomas and to Julie and Tim Dixon, their losses and pain are immeasurable. At the end of the Trial a statement by the Dixon's daughter Mrs Julie Pratley said "To many, our mum and dad are just another two faces that happened to be in the wrong place at the wrong time. But to our family they are irreplaceable – there are no words that come close to explaining the impact this has had on us. An integral part of our family is missing. Mum and dad were loving, gentle and loved people. They were also a charismatic couple who invested a lot of time and energy in their local community. They had wisdom, humour and were compassionate. Even after two decades their absence is immense and still painful." Tim Dixon added "On behalf of all those affected by this man we would like to sincerely thank DCS Steve Wilkins and his team and all the officers over the years and the forensic science services also. Today's verdict gives us justice but there is no sentence the courts could impose that would ever compensate for what we have lost and the impact the loss of mum and dad will have on the rest of our lives."

Tim Dixon, read out the following joint statement from the families of all Cooper's victims. "Whilst this cannot take away our loss and grief, and the pain of the other people touched by his violence, we can have some closure now the person responsible for these terrible atrocities has been served justice."
However, this may not be the final chapter for Cooper murder investigations. When he was sentenced the Police said in 2011 that they were looking at the other mysteries of Flo Evans death, and the double deaths at Llangolman and at Llanharry. Since then another six years has passed with no indication from the Police that any progress is being made.

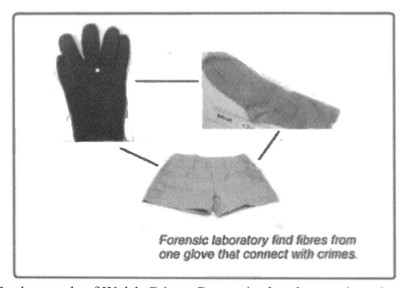

Forensic laboratory find fibres from one glove that connect with crimes.

In the annals of Welsh Crime, Cooper is already notorious, but we may find that he is involved with even more deaths. Although very unlikely, Cooper may now admit to his involvement with other deaths in South and West Wales. With the realization that he is going to remain behind bars for the rest of his life, he may consider making confessions. After all, he secretly would enjoy the limelight before a Crown Court and a jury, if only to relieve the boredom of prison life. His destiny would still be the same but being found guilty of more murders would bring closure of these mysteries which have caused such distress to so many people over a span of forty years. Cooper, who we know to be a liar and a murderer is no fool. He had his reasons to shout to the Court that evidence had been withheld. If such evidence would not implicate him with the crimes, then he should have made sure his Defence brought these factors before the Court. One can therefore assume he is is referring to such"evidence " as the cigarette butts at Scoveston, his black bicycle, his dog at the Teenage Attack and possibly a gun that was "planted" by him at Little Haven, to confuse the Dixon enquiry. These items were not brought up in his Trial. This so called 'evidence' he was waiting to refute and had answers for, but did not have the opportunity to do so. For his Defence to bring them to the Court would have indicated guilty knowledge.

Observations within this book are entirely my own. My comments are based on my locally acquired information together with that seen in the media, that read in Steve Wilkins's book, and information brought up in the two Cooper Trials. If some of my facts are incorrect or cause offence, I do apologize. I have personally known the majority of the professionals named in this book. Many families, including some of my best friends have had their lives destroyed by Cooper's actions. They refused to help me write this book, as it would resurrect memories that they desperately want to forget. It may be that they also know so much more about Cooper, that they do not want revealed.

Death Penalty.
In the UK the death penalty was formally abolished in 1965, one year after two men were executed by hanging. The son of one of these men advocates that the death penalty should still be an option. Studies have shown that Capital Punishment does not form a deterrent for murder (homicides). The last of the British executioners stated that the only reason for the death penalty is revenge. In advanced mammal societies death or ousting out of the community is how gross misdemeanours are dealt with. This happens with dolphin society and dolphins have larger brains than us.
In 2011 some 51 % favoured the death penalty but that figure is now diminishing. Innocent people have been executed and in some countries still are. In the Philippines today, the Police kill offenders and then see if there are any objections later. It saves time and money, especially when the Police have little concept of the collection of evidence or the writing of statements. The Judicial system and the Courts have little experience as they are so infrequently involved. Innocent people and petty criminals are also removed from society with these extra-judicial killings. Is President Duterte's slaughter, with innocents being killed any different to civilians being amongst those bombed in a war zone? His policy is working, despite UN objections. Cooper's Judge instead of giving him four life sentences would have given Cooper a death sentence if the option to do so was there. The outcome and the fact that Cooper is now in prison is the correct one but I firmly believe it took far too long for the evidence to be produced.

"The Pembrokeshire Murders, Catching the Bullseye Killer " by Steve
Wilkins and Jonathan Hill, by Seren Books, ISBN 07817812-800-0 is an
interesting book and well worth reading. It reads 'like a novel' is one
compliment I have heard.

The Wilkins book travels through the twists and turns of the Cooper
investigation; giving the highlights and the disappointments of the 23
years involved to reach a conviction. However as it has self praise for the
Police, it encourages me to make observations about some of their
actions or non actions. This is my alternative story of how I see events
and of how Cooper affected the County of Pembrokeshire. Although
frowned upon by the Prison Service, it would be far more intriguing if I
could encourage Cooper himself to write the next book.

Cooper is now behind bars and Dyfed Powys Police and the Judiciary
are to be congratulated for putting him there. Pembrokeshire can now,
with a big sigh of relief, revert to some sort of normality knowing that
Cooper will never be come out of prison.

A disturbing conclusion.

By covering these murders and suspected murders, we have to
acknowledge that Cooper has demonstrated a variety of killing methods
other than using a double barrelled shotgun.

I surmise he has throttled elderly persons, drowned Flo Evans, injected
air into his wife and struck Griff Thomas with a spiked hammer. Both the
judge and the profilers consider that Cooper will never confess to any of
his crimes. Now he knows he is behind bars for life, with no chance of
any reprieve, things may change. He planned most of his crimes
methodically, sometimes months in advance. However, we also know he
was unpredictable and likely to panic when he lost. Because he used a
variety of murder weapons and techniques I would not be surprised if he
did not poison Pembrokeshire people as well. The Prosecution Service is
unlikely to want to pursue his other crimes. Even if there is
overwhelming evidence, as in the case of Flo Evans, that she was
murdered by Cooper, as it is an expensive process to prove guilt and as
he is already behind bars for life, public money can be better utilised. If
everyone who knew Cooper put their heads together it would be quite
easy to contemplate many more sudden or mysterious deaths that Cooper
was responsible for.

Statistics on Accidental Deaths for Agricultural Workers, during Cooper's active years was considerably higher in Pembrokeshire than any other County in Wales. It may be an irrelevant statistic but I am sure he killed, on average, one person a year. The Police know of four separate incidents where Cooper entered a house knowing their was a female alone. He blindfolded them and tied them to a bed while he robbed their jewellery. When he departed he removed the cord and took that with him, leaving nothing but a terrified woman traumatised for the rest of her life. The Police do not tell us if rape was involved, but even if we do not know, there would have been others, so petrified of Cooper returning to kill them if they reported it, that these crimes are completely unrecorded.

Perhaps it is better if we do not search for the truth. Should we allow all his crimes to be put in the past so that this gruesome and ugly part of Pembrokeshire history is slowly forgotten?   Perhaps.

Perhaps I should not have written this book, I certainly will not gain financially from doing so. I am a Pembrokeshire historian that wanted to add my perspective of what I believe was going on with both Cooper and the twenty odd years of Police investigation. Some justice has been achieved, at a very high price, by putting inside a murderer of four people and a sexual attack. But what now should society be doing, if anything, about Cooper's other murders? And who decides? It would be far more beneficial to all if money, instead of employing detectives, was given to Cooper to write his own memoirs. The Prison Service find these ideas abhorrent, as it boosts and glorifies the egos of murderers and increases their notoriety. However, Cooper may confess his guilt to these and more unbeknown murders. Although reviving the past it would bring enormous relief and better closure to this ugly chapter in Pembrokeshire's history book.

Sources and Internet reading relating to John Cooper.

www.walesonline.co.uk/news/wales-news/2011/05/29/bizarre-drowning-of-fully-clothed-woman- in-cold-bath-looked-at-again-91466-28782319/#ixzz1XpqkbqqV

http://www.walesonline.co.uk/multimedia/pembrokeshire-murders/video/2011/05/26/john-cooper- trial-the- forensics-91466-28771745/

http://www.dailymail.co.uk/news/article-1391160/DNA-clue-nails-killer-2-couples-26- years.html#ixzz3GlQdpF9f

http://www.walesonline.co.uk/news/wales-news/2011/05/27/was-john-cooper-responsible-for- more-deaths- 91466-28775272/#ixzz1UfpgcEQp

http://www.walesonline.co.uk/multimedia/pembrokeshire-murders/video/2011/05/26/john-cooper- trial-the- investigation-91466-28771742/

Conclusion by Dyfed Powys Police

http://www.dyfed-powys.police.uk/en/news/latest-news/201105/conclusion-the-john-william- cooper-trial http://www.dyfed-powys.police.uk/en/news/latest-news/201105/what-the-conviction- cooper- means- pembrokeshire

Guardian summary of the Cooper story.

http://www.guardian.co.uk/uk/2011/may/26/john-cooper-murders-finally-solved **Mirror summary** http://www.mirror.co.uk/news/top-stories/2011/05/27/shotgun- killer-john-cooper-jailed- for-life-115875- 23159624/#ixzz1YXQUKa6p

ITV footage of Cooper on the Bulleseye Show can be seen on the internet by looking at this post http://www.itv.com/wales/the-bullseye-Killer48779/

http://www.tvforum.co.uk/forums/post708875#post-708875

The Pembrokeshire Murders Catching the Bullseye Killer, Steve Wilkins and Jonathan Hill, 2014 Seren Books ISBN 978-1-78172-800-0

The Game Show Killer, More Pembrokeshire Murders. JK Rogers, e-book Amazon 2017

Printed in Great Britain
by Amazon